The Shakespeare Birthday Book

William Shakespeare

In the interest of creating a more extensive selection of rare historical book reprints, we have chosen to reproduce this title even though it may possibly have occasional imperfections such as missing and blurred pages, missing text, poor pictures, markings, dark backgrounds and other reproduction issues beyond our control. Because this work is culturally important, we have made it available as a part of our commitment to protecting, preserving and promoting the world's literature. Thank you for your understanding.

THE SHAKESPEARE BIRTHDAY BOOK.

*"My blessing with thee,
and these few precepts in thy memory."*
Hamlet, Act 1. Sc. 3.

SHAKESPEARE'S BIRTHPLACE
STRATFORD ON AVON

LONDON
HATCHARDS, PICCADILLY.
1876.

All rights reserved.

Malone A. 57.

SHAKESPEARE.
BORN 1564   DIED 1616.
THE "CHANDOS" PORTRAIT.

DEDICATED

(BY PERMISSION)

TO

HER ROYAL HIGHNESS

THE PRINCESS MARY ADELAIDE,

DUCHESS OF TECK.

THE NEW YEAR.

LEAVING our rankness and irregular course,
Stoop low within those bounds we have o'erlooked,
And calmly run on in obedience,
. . . Away, my friends! New flight;
And happy newness, that intends old right.

King John, Act v. Sc. 4.

SHAKESPEARE'S COURTSHIP.

JANUARY.

When icicles hang by the wall,
   And Dick the shepherd blows his nail,
And Tom bears logs into the hall,
   And milk comes frozen home in pail,
     *   *   *   *   *
When all aloud the wind doth blow,
And birds sit brooding in the snow.

Love's Labour's Lost, Act v. Sc. 2.

Sometimes hath the brightest day a cloud;
And after summer evermore succeeds
Barren winter, with his wrathful nipping cold:
So cares and joys abound, as seasons fleet.

Second Part of Henry VI. Act II. Sc. 4.

─── *January 1.* ───

Go thou forth;
And fortune play upon thy prosperous helm.
All's Well that Ends Well, Act III. Sc. 3.

In the great hand of God I stand.
Macbeth, Act II. Sc. 3.

─── *January 2.* ───

Let us not burden our remembrance with
A heaviness that's gone.
Tempest, Act V. Sc. 1.

We thought there was no more behind,
But such a day to-morrow as to-day,
And to be boy eternal.
Winter's Tale, Act I. Sc. 2.

─── *January 3.* ───

Courage and comfort! all shall yet go well.
King John, Act III. Sc. 4.

Defer no time, delays have dangerous ends.
First Part of Henry VI. Act III. Sc. 2.

Pleasure and action make the hours seem short.
Othello, Act II. Sc. 3.

January 1.

January 2.

January 3.

January 4.

Sure, He that made us with such large discourse,
Looking before and after, gave us not
That capability and God-like reason
To fust in us unused. *Hamlet*, Act. IV. Sc. 4.

Let the end try the man.
Second Part of Henry IV. Act II. Sc. 2.

Stay yet another day, thou trusty Welshman.
Richard II. Act II. Sc. 4.

January 5.

Let our old acquaintance be renewed.
Second Part of Henry IV. Act III. Sc. 2.

Be patient, for the world is broad and wide.
Romeo and Juliet, Act III. Sc. 3.

January 6.

Thanks, fortune, yet, that, after all my crosses,
Thou givest me somewhat to repair myself.
Pericles, Act II. Sc. 1.

I have immortal longings in me.
Antony and Cleopatra, Act V. Sc. 2.

January 4.

January 5.

January 6.

——————— *January 7.* ———————

Lay aside life-harming heaviness,
And entertain a cheerful disposition.
Richard II. Act II. Sc. 2.

A trusty villain, sir, that very oft
When I am dull with care and melancholy,
Lightens my humour with his merry jests.
Comedy of Errors, Act I. Sc. 2.

——————— *January 8.* ———————

The expectancy and rose of this fair state.
Hamlet, Act III. Sc. 1.

The Lord bless you!
God prosper your affairs! God send us peace!
Second Part of Henry IV. Act III. Sc. 2.

——————— *January 9.* ———————

Thy life is dear; for all that life can rate
Worth name of life in thee hath estimate,
Youth, beauty, wisdom, courage, all
That happiness and prime can happy call.
All's Well that Ends Well, Act II. Sc. 1.

No legacy is so rich as honesty.
All's Well that Ends Well, Act III. Sc. 5.

January 7.

January 8.

January 9.

4

January 10.

Your gentleness shall force
More than your force move us to gentleness.
As You Like It, Act II. Sc. 7.

Truth hath a quiet breast.
Richard II. Act I. Sc. 3.

January 11.

We, ignorant of ourselves,
Beg often our own harms, which the wise powers
Deny us for our good; so find we profit
By losing of our prayers.
Antony and Cleopatra, Act II. Sc. 1.

Here comes a man of comfort, whose advice
Hath often stilled my brawling discontent.
Measure for Measure, Act IV. Sc. 1.

January 12.

Love, give me strength! and strength shall help afford.
Romeo and Juliet, Act IV. Sc. 1.

Amen, if you love her, for the lady is very well worthy.
Much Ado about Nothing, Act I. Sc. 1.

January 10.

January 11.

January 12.

January 13.

The means that heaven yields must be embraced,
And not neglected; else, if Heaven would
And we will not, Heaven's offer we refuse,
The proffered means of succour and redress.
Richard II. Act III. Sc. 2.

A man of good repute, carriage, bearing, and estimation.
Love's Labour's Lost, Act I. Sc. 1.

January 14.

What, gone without a word?
Ay, so true love should do: it cannot speak;
For truth hath better deeds than words to grace it.
Two Gentlemen of Verona, Act II. Sc. 2.

Thou should'st not have been old till thou hadst been wise.
King Lear, Act I. Sc. 5.

January 15.

O, that a man might know
The end of this day's business ere it come!
But it sufficeth that the day will end,
And then the end is known
Julius Cæsar, Act V. Sc. 1.

Kindness in women, not their beauteous looks, shall win my love.
Taming of the Shrew, Act V. Sc. 2.

———————— *January 13.* ————————

———————— *January 14.* ————————

———————— *January 15.* ————————

January 16.

Happy thou art not;
For what thou hast not, still thou strivest to get,
And what thou hast, forget'st.
Measure for Measure, Act III. Sc. 1.

And seek for sorrow with thy spectacles.
Second Part of Henry VI. Act V. Sc. 1.

January 17.

How oft the sight of means to do ill deeds
Make deeds ill done.
King John, Act IV. Sc. 2.

O time! thou must untangle this, not I;
It is too hard a knot for me to untie!
Twelfth Night, Act II. Sc. 2.

January 18.

What stature is she of?
Just as high as my heart.
As You Like It, Act III. Sc. 2.

He hath an excellent good name.
Much Ado about Nothing, Act III. Sc. 1.

Every why hath a wherefore.
Comedy of Errors, Act II. Sc. 2.

January 16.

January 17.

January 18.

―――――― *January 19.* ――――――

Cannot a plain man live, and think no harm?
Richard III. Act I. Sc. 3.

Well, I am not fair; and therefore I pray the gods make me honest.
As You Like It, Act III. Sc. 3.

―――――― *January 20.* ――――――

Heaven bless thee!
Thou hast the sweetest face I ever looked on.
Henry VIII. Act IV. Sc. 1.

A friend should bear his friend's infirmities.
Julius Cæsar, Act IV. Sc. 3.

―――――― *January 21.* ――――――

If thou art rich, thou art poor;
For like an ass whose back with ingots bows,
Thou bear'st thy heavy riches but a journey,
And death unloads thee.
Measure for Measure, Act III. Sc. 1.

It is as hard to come as for a camel
To thread the postern of a small needle's eye.
Richard II. Act V. Sc. 5.

14

January 19.

January 20.

January 21.

─── *January 22.* ───

The dearest friend to me, the kindest man,
The best condition'd and unwearied spirit
In doing courtesies.
     Merchant of Venice, Act III. Sc. 2.

Teach thy necessity to reason thus:
There is no virtue like necessity.
     Richard II. Act I. Sc. 3.

─── *January 23.* ───

He will keep that good name still.
     Henry V. Act III. Sc. 7.

We carry not a heart with us from hence,
That grows not in a fair consent with ours,
Nor leave not one behind, that doth not wish
Success and conquest to attend on us.
     Henry V. Act II. Sc. 2.

─── *January 24.* ───

I swear he is truehearted, and a soul
None better in my kingdom.
     Henry VIII. Act V. Sc. 1.

They have seemed to be together, though absent;
shook hands, as over a vast.
     Winter's Tale, Act I. Sc. 1.

January 22.

January 23.

January 24.

January 25.

Men at some time are masters of their fates:
The fault, dear Brutus, is not in our stars,
But in ourselves.
Julius Cæsar, Act I. Sc. 2.

God amend us, God amend! We are much out o' the way.
Love's Labour's Lost, Act IV. Sc. 3.

January 26.

But I'll endeavour deeds to match these words.
Troilus and Cressida, Act IV. Sc. 5.

I am Sir Oracle,
And, when I ope my lips, let no dog bark.
Merchant of Venice, Act I. Sc. 1.

January 27.

I like your silence, it the more shows off
Your wonder. *Winter's Tale,* Act V. Sc. 3.

Be to yourself
As you would to your friend.
Henry VIII. Act I. Sc. 1.

Affliction may one day smile again: and till then, sit thee down, Sorrow!
Love's Labour's Lost, Act I. Sc. 1.

January 25.

January 26.

January 27.

January 28.

'Tis not the many oaths that make the truth,
But the plain single vow that's vowed true.
All's Well that Ends Well, Act IV. Sc. 2.

I have heard of the lady, and good words went with her name.
Measure for Measure, Act III. Sc. 1.

January 29.

As much good stay with thee as go with me.
Richard II. Act I. Sc. 2.

In faith honest as the skin between his brows.
Much Ado about Nothing, Act III. Sc. 5.

January 30.

You have deserved
High commendation, true applause, and love.
As You Like It, Act I. Sc. 2.

New customs,
Though they be never so ridiculous,
Nay, let 'em be unmanly, yet are followed.
Henry VIII. Act I. Sc. 3.

January 28.

January 29.

January 30.

January 31.

His years but young, but his experience old:
His head unmellowed, but his judgment ripe.
Two Gentlemen of Verona, Act II. Sc. 4.

God . . send him many years of sunshine days!
Richard II. Act IV. Sc. 1.

Of all say'd yet, may'st thou prove prosperous.
Of all say'd yet, I wish thee happiness.
Pericles, Act I. Sc. 1.

January 31.

SHAKESPEARE BROUGHT BEFORE SIR THOMAS LUCY.

FEBRUARY.

THE seasons alter: hoary-headed frosts
Fall in the fresh lap of the crimson rose,
And on old Hiems' thin and icy crown
An odorous chaplet of sweet summer buds
Is, as in mockery, set: the spring, the summer,
The childing autumn, angry winter, change
Their wonted liveries, and the mazed world,
By their increase, now knows not which is which.
Midsummer Night's Dream, Act II. Sc. I.

Call it winter, which being full of care
Makes summer's welcome thrice more wish'd, more
   rare.
Sonnet LVI.

February 1.

For there is nothing either good or bad, but thinking makes it so.
Hamlet, Act II. Sc. 2.

Virtue is bold, and goodness never fearful.
Measure for Measure, Act III. Sc. 1.

February 2.

If reasons were as plentiful as blackberries, I would give no man a reason upon compulsion, I.
First Part of Henry IV. Act II. Sc. 4.

In faith, he is a worthy gentleman,
Exceedingly well read.
First Part of Henry IV. Act III. Sc. 1.

February 3.

What fates impose, that men must needs abide;
It boots not to resist both wind and tide.
Third Part of Henry VI. Act IV. Sc. 3.

Constant you are,
But yet a woman, and for secrecy
No lady closer, for I well believe
Thou wilt not utter what thou dost not know.
First Part of Henry IV. Act II. Sc. 3.

February 1.

February 2.

February 3.

February 4.

I would applaud thee to the very echo,
That should applaud again.
Macbeth, Act V. Sc. 3.

O ye gods, render me worthy of this noble wife.
Julius Cæsar, Act II. Sc. 1.

February 5.

Let's carry with us ears and eyes for the time,
But hearts for the event.
Coriolanus, Act II. Sc. 1.

They say best men are moulded out of faults.
Measure for Measure, Act V. Sc. 1.

February 6.

Why, what's the matter,
That you have such a February face,
So full of frost, of storm, and cloudiness?
Much Ado about Nothing, Act V. Sc. 4.

What's gone and what's past help
Should be past grief.
Winter's Tale, Act III. Sc. 2.

February 4.

February 5.

February 6.

―――― *February 7.* ――――

Men shall deal unadvisedly sometimes,
Which after hours give leisure to repent.
Richard III. Act IV. Sc. 4.

Our contentment is our best having.
Henry VIII. Act II. Sc. 3.

―――― *February 8.* ――――

Neither a borrower nor a lender be;
For loan oft loses both itself and friend,
And borrowing dulls the edge of husbandry.
Hamlet, Act I. Sc. 3.

Yet I do fear thy nature,
It is too full o' the milk of human kindness.
Macbeth, Act I. Sc. 5.

―――― *February 9.* ――――

One touch of nature makes the whole world kin.
Troilus and Cressida, Act III. Sc. 3.

Grace and remembrance be to you both.
Winter's Tale, Act IV. Sc. 4.

It is not enough to speak, but to speak true.
Midsummer Night's Dream, Act V. Sc. 1.

February 7.

February 8.

February 9.

February 10.

Let myself and fortune
Tug for the time to come.
Winter's Tale, Act IV. Sc. 4.

I do not know that Englishman alive
With whom my soul is any jot at odds.
Richard III. Act II. Sc. 1.

February 11.

God has given you one face, and you make yourselves another.
Hamlet, Act III. Sc. 1.

Those friends thou hast, and their adoption tried,
Grapple them to thy soul with hoops of steel.
Hamlet, Act I. Sc. 3.

February 12.

I will chide no breather in the world but myself, against whom I know most faults.
As You Like it, Act III. Sc. 2.

Thus, Indian-like,
Religious in mine error, I adore.
All's Well that Ends Well, Act I. Sc. 3.

February 10.

February 11.

February 12.

February 13.

But I am constant as the northern star,
Of whose true-fix'd and resting quality
There is no fellow in the firmament.
Julius Cæsar, Act III. Sc. 1.

She's a good creature.
Merry Wives, Act II. Sc. 2.

February 14.

(ST. VALENTINE.)

. . . Sleep in peace and wake in joy;
Good angels guard thee. *Richard III.* Act V. Sc. 3.

I know no ways to mince it in love, but directly to say—I love you. *Henry V.* Act V. Sc. 2.

Doubt thou the stars are fire;
 Doubt that the sun doth move;
Doubt truth to be a liar;
 But never doubt I love. *Hamlet*, Act II. Sc. 2.

February 15.

Be sure of this,
What I can help thee to thou shalt not miss.
All's Well that Ends Well, Act I. Sc. 3.

Be stirring as the time; be fire with fire;
. . . . so shall inferior eyes

. . . . . .

Grow great by your example, and put on
The dauntless spirit of resolution.
King John, Act V. Sc. 1.

February 13.

February 14.

February 15.

February 16.

'Tis much he dares;
And, to that dauntless temper of his mind,
He hath a wisdom that doth guide his valour
To act in safety.
Macbeth, Act III. Sc. 1.

She is a woman, therefore may be woo'd;
She is a woman, therefore may be won.
Titus Andronicus, Act II. Sc. 1.

February 17.

Love sought is good, but given unsought is better.
Twelfth Night, Act III. Sc. 1.

Methinks thou art more honest now than wise.
Timon of Athens, Act IV. Sc. 3.

February 18.

O, this boy,
Lends metal to us all!
First Part of Henry IV. Act V. Sc. 4.

Who steals my purse steals trash;
'Twas mine, 'tis his, and has been slave to thousands;
But he that filches from me my good name
Robs me of that which not enriches him
And makes me poor indeed. *Othello*, Act III. Sc. 3.

February 16.

February 17.

February 18.

February 19.

Let fancy still my sense in Lethe steep;
If it be thus to dream, still let me sleep!
Twelfth Night, Act IV. Sc. 1.

Look, what is best, that best I wish in thee.
Sonnet XXXVII.

February 20.

Her whose worth makes other worthies nothing.
She is alone.
Two Gentlemen of Verona, Act II. Sc. 4.

Let Hercules himself do what he may,
The cat will mew, and dog will have his day.
Hamlet, Act V. Sc. 1.

February 21.

God in heaven bless thee!
Romeo and Juliet, Act II. Sc. 4.

How far that little candle throws his beams!
So shines a good deed in a naughty world.
Merchant of Venice, Act V. Sc. 1.

February 19.

February 20.

February 21.

―――― *February 22.* ――――

From lowest place when virtuous things proceed,
The place is dignified by the doer's deed.
All's Well that Ends Well, Act II. Sc. 3.

He that wants money, means, and content, is without three good friends.
As You Like It, Act III. Sc. 2.

―――― *February 23.* ――――

Do as the heavens have done, forget your evil;
With them forgive yourself.
Winter's Tale, Act V. Sc. 1.

Whereto serves mercy
But to confront the visage of offence?
And what's in prayer but this two-fold force,
To be forestalled ere we come to fall,
Or pardon'd being down? Then I'll look up;
My fault is past. But, O, what form of prayer
Can serve my turn? *Hamlet*, Act III. Sc. 3.

―――― *February 24.* ――――

For now he lives in fame, though not in life.
Richard III. Act III. Sc. 1.

All places that the eye of Heaven visits
Are to a wise man ports and happy havens.
Richard II. Act I. Sc. 3.

A greater power than we can contradict
Hath thwarted our intents.
Romeo and Juliet, Act V. Sc. 3.

February 22.

February 23.

February 24.

───── *February 25.* ─────

Thou see'st we are not all alone unhappy:
This wide and universal theatre
Presents more woeful pageants than the scene
Wherein we play in. *As You Like It*, Act II. Sc. 7.

It never yet did hurt
To lay down likelihoods and forms of hope.
Second Part of Henry IV. Act I. Sc. 3.

───── *February 26.* ─────

Nothing do I see in you
That I can find should merit any hate.
King John, Act II. Sc. 1.

But where the greater malady is fixed,
The lesser is scarce felt.
King Lear, Act III. Sc. 4.

───── *February 27.* ─────

It is the purpose that makes strong the vow;
But vows to every purpose must not hold.
Troilus and Cressida, Act V. Sc. 3.

Day serves not light more faithful than I'll be.
Pericles, Act I. Sc. 2.

February 25.

February 26.

February 27.

February 28.

And those about her
From her shall read the perfect ways of honour.
Henry VIII. Act v. Sc. 5.

Fortune reigns in gifts of the world, not in the lineaments of nature.
As You Like It, Act I. Sc. 2.

February 29.

And yet, good faith, I wish'd myself a man,
Or that we women had men's privilege
Of speaking first. *Troilus and Cressida,* Act III. Sc. 2.

Let men take heed of their company.
Second Part of Henry IV. Act v. Sc. 1.

If it were done when 'tis done, then 'twere well
It were done quickly. *Macbeth,* Act I. Sc. 7.

February 28.

February 29.

THE MERCHANT OF VENICE.
ACT 2 SCENE 5

MARCH.

When daffodils begin to peer,
  With heigh! the doxy over the dale,
Why, then comes in the sweet o' the year;
  For the red blood reigns in the Winter's pale.
Winter's Tale, Act IV. Sc. 3.

Daffodils, that come before the swallow dares,
And take the winds of March with beauty.
Winter's Tale, Act IV. Sc. 4.

Now 'tis the spring, and weeds are shallow-rooted;
Suffer them now, and they'll o'ergrow the garden
And choke the herbs for want of husbandry.
Second Part of Henry VI. Act III. Sc. 1.

March 1.
(St. David's Day.)
And I do believe your Majesty takes no scorn
to wear the leek upon Saint Tavy's Day.
Henry V. Act IV. Sc. 7.

Joy, gentle friends! joy and fresh days of love
Accompany your hearts!
Midsummer Night's Dream, Act V. Sc. 1.

Though it appear a little out of fashion,
There is much care and valour in this Welshman.
Henry V. Act IV. Sc. 1.

March 2.
A man that I love and honour with my soul, and
my heart, and my duty, and my life, and my living,
and my uttermost power: . . . I think in my very
conscience he is as valiant a man as Mark Antony;
and he is a man of no estimation in the world.
Henry V. Act III. Sc. 6.

Exceeding wise, fair-spoken, and persuading.
Henry VIII. Act IV. Sc. 2.

March 3.
I am amazed, methinks, and lose my way
Among the thorns and dangers of this world.
King John, Act IV. Sc. 3.

It pleases time and fortune to lie heavy
Upon a friend of mine, who, in hot blood,
Hath stepp'd into the law, which is past depth
To those that, without heed, do plunge into't.
Timon of Athens, Act III. Sc. 5.

———— *March 1.* ————

———— *March 2.* ————

———— *March 3.* ————

March 4.

Valiant as a lion,
And wondrous affable, and as bountiful
As mines of India.
First Part of Henry IV. Act III. Sc. 1.

I this infer,—
That many things, having full reference
To one consent, may work contrariously.
Henry V. Act I. Sc. 2.

March 5.

Still in thy right hand carry gentle peace,
To silence envious tongues.
Henry VIII. Act III. Sc. 2.

And she is fair, and, fairer than that word,
Of wondrous virtues.
Merchant of Venice, Act I. Sc. 1.

March 6.

Ever beloved and loving may his rule be!
And when old time shall lead him to his end,
Goodness and he fill up one monument.
Henry VIII. Act II. Sc. 1.

I pray thee sort thy heart to patience.
Second Part of Henry VI. Act II. Sc. 4.

March 4.

March 5.

March 6.

―――― *March 7.* ――――

Since this fortune falls to you,
Be content and seek no new.
Merchant of Venice, Act III. Sc. 2.

Be as thou wast wont to be;
See as thou wast wont to see.
Midsummer Night's Dream, Act IV. Sc. 1.

―――― *March 8.* ――――

Ill blows the wind that profits nobody.
Third Part of Henry VI. Act II. Sc. 5.

'Tis better to be lowly born,
And range with humble livers in content,
Than to be perk'd up in a glistering grief
And wear a golden sorrow.
Henry VIII. Act II. Sc. 3.

―――― *March 9.* ――――

Oft expectation fails, and most oft there
Where most it promises; and oft it hits
Where hope is coldest and despair most fits.
All's Well that Ends Well, Act II. Sc. 1.

I have a man's mind, but a woman's might.
Julius Cæsar, Act II. Sc. 4.

March 7.

March 8.

March 9.

―――― *March 10.* ――――

Honour, riches, marriage-blessing,
Long continuance, and increasing,
Hourly joys be still upon you!
Juno sings her blessings on you.

Tempest, Act IV. Sc. 1.

God be wi' you, with all my heart.

Troilus and Cressida, Act III. Sc. 3.

―――― *March 11.* ――――

O Lady Fortune, stand you auspicious!

Winter's Tale, Act IV. Sc. 4.

Hereafter, in a better world than this,
I shall desire more love and knowledge of you.

As You Like It, Act I. Sc. 2.

―――― *March 12.* ――――

Ay, sir; to be honest, as this world goes, is to be one man picked out of ten thousand.

Hamlet, Act II. Sc. 2.

But there's more in me than thou understand'st.

Troilus and Cressida, Act IV. Sc. 5.

March 10.

March 11.

March 12.

―――― *March 13.* ――――

Sir, I am a true labourer, I earn that I get, get that I wear, owe no man hate, envy no man's happiness.
As You Like It, Act III. Sc. 2.

Sweet flowers are slow, and weeds make haste.
Richard III. Act II. Sc. 4.

―――― *March 14.* ――――

For truth is truth, to the end of the reckoning.
Measure for Measure, Act V. Sc. 1.

I do beseech you—
Chiefly that I might set it in my prayers—
What is your name?
Tempest, Act III. Sc. 1.

―――― *March 15.* ――――

Beware the ides of March.
Julius Cæsar, Act I. Sc. 2.

How poor are they that have not patience!
What wound did ever heal but by degrees?
Othello, Act II. Sc. 3.

To be in anger is impiety;
But who is man that is not angry?
Timon of Athens, Act III. Sc. 5

March 13.

March 14.

March 15.

March 16.

What touches us ourself should be last served.
Julius Cæsar, Act III. Sc. 1.

It is the bright day that brings forth the adder;
And that craves wary walking.
Julius Cæsar, Act II. Sc. 1.

March 17.

(St. Patrick's Day.)

Altogether directed by an Irishman; a very valiant gentleman, i' faith.
Henry V. Act III. Sc. 2.

'Tis not enough to help the feeble up,
But to support him after. Fare you well.
All happiness to your honour!
Timon of Athens, Act I. Sc. 1.

March 18.

Women will love her, that she is a woman
More worth than any man; men, that she is
The rarest of all women.
Winter's Tale, Act V. Sc. 1.

He that is giddy thinks the world turns round.
Taming of the Shrew, Act V. Sc. 2.

March 16.

March 17.

March 18.

March 19.

When love begins to sicken and decay,
It useth an enforced ceremony.
There are no tricks in plain and simple faith.

Julius Cæsar, Act IV. Sc. 2.

Why should I then be false, since it is true
That I must die here and live hence by truth?

King John, Act V. Sc. 4.

March 20.

For I profess not talking; only this—
Let each man do his best.

First Part of Henry IV. Act V. Sc. 3.

That ever this fellow should have fewer words than a parrot, and yet the son of a woman!

First Part of Henry IV. Act II. Sc. 4.

March 21.

Firm of word,
Speaking in deeds and deedless in his tongue;
Not soon provoked nor being provoked soon calm'd;
His heart and hand both open and both free.

Troilus and Cressida, Act IV. Sc. 5.

What cannot be eschewed, must be embraced.

Merry Wives of Windsor, Act V. Sc. 5.

March 19.

March 20.

March 21.

———————— *March 22.* ————————

That what we have we prize not to the worth
Whiles we enjoy it, but being lack'd and lost
Why, then we rack the value, then we find
The virtue that possession would not show us
Whiles it was ours.
Much Ado about Nothing, Act IV. Sc. 1.

My bosom is full of kindness.
Twelfth Night, Act II. Sc. 1.

———————— *March 23.* ————————

There's a special providence in the fall of a sparrow.
Hamlet, Act V. Sc. 2.

Society is no comfort to one not sociable.
Cymbeline, Act IV. Sc. 2.

———————— *March 24.* ————————

She is an earthly paragon.
Two Gentlemen of Verona, Act II. Sc. 4.

If he serve God,
We'll serve Him too and be his fellow so.
Richard II. Act III. Sc. 2.

Time is the king of men,
He's both their parent, and he is their grave,
And gives them what he will, not what they crave.
Pericles, Act II. Sc. 3.

March 22.

March 23.

March 24.

March 25.

While I remain above the ground, you shall
Hear from me still, and never of me aught
But what is like me formerly.

Coriolanus, Act IV. Sc. 1.

The gentleness of all the gods go with thee.

Twelfth Night, Act II. Sc. 1.

March 26.

A soldier firm, and sound of heart.

Henry V. Act III. Sc. 6.

Truth shall nurse her,
Holy and heavenly thoughts still counsel her:
She shall be loved and feared: her own shall bless her.

Henry VIII. Act V. Sc. 5.

Of many good I think him best.

Two Gentlemen of Verona, Act I. Sc. 2.

March 27.

The world is full of rubs.

Richard II. Act III. Sc. 4.

This world is not for aye.

Hamlet, Act III. Sc. 2.

Since the affairs of men rest still uncertain,
Let's reason with the worst that may befall.

Julius Cæsar, Act V. Sc. 1.

March 25.

March 26.

March 27.

March 28.

Thou art e'en as just a man
As e'er my conversation coped withal.
Hamlet, Act III. Sc. 2.

Many days shall see her,
And yet no day without a deed to crown it.
Henry VIII. Act V. Sc. 5.

Death lies on her like an untimely frost
Upon the sweetest flower of all the field. . . .
Romeo and Juliet, Act IV. Sc. 5.

March 29.

There are more things in heaven and earth
Than are dreamt of in your philosophy.
Hamlet, Act I. Sc. 5.

He loves his own barn better than he loves our house.
First Part of Henry IV. Act II. Sc. 3.

March 30.

Nature, what things there are,
Most abject in regard and dear in use!
What things again most dear in the esteem
And poor in worth!
Troilus and Cressida, Act III. Sc. 3.

And now am I, if a man should speak truly,
little better than one of the wicked.
First Part of Henry IV. Act I. Sc. 2.

March 28.

March 29.

March 30.

March 31.

Not fearing death, nor shrinking for distress,
But always resolute in most extremes.
First Part of Henry VI. Act IV. Sc. 1.

But how long fairly shall her sweet life last?
So long as Heaven, and Nature lengthens it.
Richard III. Act IV. Sc. 4.

March 31

THE TAMING OF THE SHREW.
ACT 4. SCENE 3.

APRIL.

When proud-pied April, dress'd in all his trim,
Hath put a spirit of youth in everything.

Sonnet XCVIII.

When daisies pied, and violets blue,
   And lady-smocks all silver-white,
And cuckoo buds of yellow hue,
   Do paint the meadows with delight.

Love's Labour's Lost, Act V. Sc. 2.

That strain again ;—it had a dying fall :
O, it came o'er my ear like the sweet south
That breathes upon a bank of violets,
Stealing and giving odour!

Twelfth Night, Act I. Sc. 1.

─────────── *April 1.* ───────────

O how this spring of love resembleth
The uncertain glory of an April day ;
Which now shows all the beauty of the sun,
And by-and-by a cloud takes all away !
Two Gentlemen of Verona, Act I. Sc. 3.

Jaq. By my troth, I was seeking for a fool when I found you.

Orl. He is drowned in the brook, look but in and you shall see him.
As You Like It, Act III. Sc. 2.

─────────── *April 2.* ───────────

Are these things then necessities?
Then let us meet them like necessities.
Second Part of Henry IV, Act III. Sc. 1.

I embrace this fortune patiently,
Since, not to be avoided, it falls on me.
First Part of Henry IV. Act v. Sc. 5.

─────────── *April 3.* ───────────

Be that you seem, truly your country's friend,
And temperately proceed to what you would.
Coriolanus, Act III. Sc. 1.

Why, nothing comes amiss, so money comes withal.
Taming of the Shrew, Act I. Sc. 2.

April 1.

April 2.

April 3.

April 4.

· So grace and mercy at your most need help you.
Hamlet, Act I. Sc. 5.

Every time serves for the matter that is then born in it.
Antony and Cleopatra, Act II. Sc. 2.

April 5.

More such days as these to us befall!
Second Part of Henry VI. Act v. Sc. 3.

O call back yesterday, bid time return.
Richard II. Act III. Sc. 2.

April 6.

All happiness bechance to thee!
Two Gentlemen of Verona, Act I. Sc. 1.

If we do now make our atonement well,
Our peace will, like a broken limb united,
Grow stronger for the breaking.
Second Part of Henry IV. Act IV. Sc. 1.

———— *April 4.* ————

———— *April 5.* ————

———— *April 6.* ————

April 7.

Who is it that says most? which can say more
Than this rich praise, that you alone are you?
Sonnet LXXXIV.

A kind overflow of kindness: there are no faces truer than those that are so washed.
Much Ado about Nothing, Act I. Sc. I.

April 8.

A learned spirit, of human dealings.
Othello, Act III. Sc. 3.

If all the year were playing holidays,
To sport would be as tedious as to work;
But when they seldom come, they wished for come.
First Part of Henry IV. Act I. Sc. 2.

April 9.

God's benison go with you; and with those
That would make good of bad, and friends of foes!
Macbeth, Act II. Sc. 4.

An angel is like you, Kate, and you are like an angel.
Henry V. Act V. Sc. 2.

April 7.

April 8.

April 9.

―――――― *April 10.* ――――――

We are such stuff
As dreams are made on ; and our little life
Is rounded with a sleep.
Tempest, Act IV. Sc. 1.

I could have better spared a better man.
First Part of Henry IV, Act V. Sc. 4.

―――――― *April 11.* ――――――

A merrier man,
Within the limit of becoming mirth,
I never spent an hour's talk withal.
Love's Labour's Lost, Act II. Sc. 1.

Experience is by industry achieved,
And perfected by the swift course of time.
Two Gentlemen of Verona, Act I. Sc. 3.

―――――― *April 12.* ――――――

More is thy due than more than all can pay.
Macbeth, Act I. Sc. 4.

By my troth, Nerissa, my little body is a-weary of this great world.
Merchant of Venice, Act I. Sc. 2.

Life is as tedious as a twice-told tale.
King John, Act III. Sc. 4.

April 10.

April 11.

April 12.

April 13.

. . . All of us have cause
To wail the dimming of our shining star;
But none can cure their harms by wailing them.
Richard III. Act II. Sc. 2.

I cannot flatter; I do defy
The tongues of soothers; but a braver place
In my heart's love hath no man than yourself.
First Part of Henry IV. Act IV. Sc. 1.

April 14.

Fair thoughts and happy hours attend on you!
Merchant of Venice, Act III. Sc. 4.

I very well agree with you in the hopes of him: it is a gallant child; one that indeed physics the subject, makes old hearts fresh: they that went on crutches ere he was born desire yet their life to see him a man.
Winter's Tale, Act I. Sc. 1.

April 15.

He was gentle but unfortunate;
Dishonestly afflicted, but yet honest.
Cymbeline, Act IV. Sc. 2.

What cannot be avoided,
'Twere childish weakness to lament or fear.
Third Part of Henry VI. Act V. Sc. 4.

April 13.

April 14.

April 15.

April 16.

This above all, to thine own self be true,
And it must follow as the night the day,
Thou canst not then be false to any man.
Hamlet, Act I. Sc. 3.

The mind much sufferance doth o'erskip,
When grief hath mates, and bearing fellowship.
King Lear, Act III. Sc. 6.

April 17.

Time hath, my lord, a wallet at his back,
Wherein he puts alms for oblivion,
A great-sized monster of ingratitudes.
Troilus and Cressida, Act III. Sc. 3.

By-and-by is easily said.
Hamlet, Act III. Sc. 2.

April 18.

He was a man, take him for all in all,
I shall not look upon his like again.
Hamlet, Act I. Sc. 2.

We are not the first
Who, with best meaning, have incurred the worst.
King Lear, Act V. Sc. 3.

O, father Abbot,
An old man, broken with the storms of state,
Is come to lay his weary bones among ye;
Give him a little earth for charity.
Henry VIII. Act IV. Sc. 2.

April 16.

April 17.

April 18.

―――― *April 19.* ――――

Our kindred, though they be long ere they are wooed, they are constant being won.

Troilus and Cressida, Act III. Sc. 2.

I am as honest as any man living that is an old man, and no honester than I.

Much Ado about Nothing, Act III. Sc. 5.

―――― *April 20.* ――――

For naught so vile that on the earth doth live
But to the earth some special good doth give.

Romeo and Juliet, Act II. Sc. 3.

How far can I praise him?

Much Ado about Nothing, Act I. Sc. 1.

―――― *April 21.* ――――

Let me be ignorant, and in nothing good,
But graciously to know I am no better.

Measure for Measure, Act II. Sc. 4.

. . . . I know the gentleman
To be of worth and worthy estimation,
And not without desert so well reputed.

Two Gentlemen of Verona, Act II. Sc. 3.

April 19.

April 20.

April 21.

April 22.

O, he's the very soul of bounty.
Timon of Athens, Act I. Sc. 2.

What's in a name? That which we call a rose,
By any other name would smell as sweet.
Romeo and Juliet, Act II. Sc. 2.

April 23.

(St. George's Day.)

This happy breed of men, this little world,
This precious stone set in the silver sea,
This land of such dear souls, this dear, dear land.
Richard II. Act II. Sc. 1.

Where'er I wander, boast of this I can,
Though banished, yet a true-born Englishman.
Richard II. Act I. Sc. 3.

April 24.

And I feel within me
A peace above all earthly dignities,
A still and quiet conscience . . . .
My hopes in heaven do dwell.
Henry VIII. Act III. Sc. 2.

I must have patience to endure the load.
Richard III. Act III. Sc. 7.

April 22.

April 23.

April 24.

―― *April 25.* ――

The heavens give safety to your purposes !
Lead forth and bring you back in happiness !
Measure for Measure, Act I. Sc. I.

Out of this nettle, danger, we pluck this flower, safety.
First Part of Henry IV. Act II. Sc. 3.

―― *April 26.* ――

Remember this,
God and our good cause fight upon our side.
Richard III. Act V. Sc. 3.

Smooth runs the water where the brook is deep.
Second Part of Henry VI. Act III. Sc. I.

―― *April 27.* ――

Our wills and fates do so contrary run
That our devices still are overthrown ;
Our thoughts are ours, their ends none of our own.
Hamlet, Act III. Sc. 2.

Sleeping neglection doth betray to loss.
First Part of Henry VI. Act IV. Sc. 3.

April 25.

April 26.

April 27.

April 28.

I never did repent for doing good,
Nor shall not now.
Merchant of Venice, Act III. Sc. 4.

Sleep that knits up the ravell'd sleeve of care,
The death of each day's life, sore labour's bath,
Balm of hurt minds, great nature's second course,
Chief nourisher in life's feast.
Macbeth, Act II. Sc. 2.

April 29.

Be patient till the last.
Julius Cæsar, Act III. Sc. 2.

Our life, exempt from public haunt,
Finds tongues in trees, books in the running brooks,
Sermons in stones, and good in everything.
As You Like It, Act II. Sc. 1.

April 30.

Before the times of change, still is it so:
By a divine instinct men's minds mistrust
Ensuing dangers; as, by proof, we see
The waters swell before a boist'rous storm,
But leave it all to God.
Richard III. Act II. Sc. 3.

The April's in her eyes: it is love's spring,
And these the showers to bring it on.
Antony and Cleopatra, Act III. Sc. 2.

April 28.

April 29.

April 30.

KING LEAR.
ACT 4. SCENE 7

M A Y.

As it fell upon a day
In the merry month of May,
Sitting in a pleasant shade
Which a grove of myrtles made,
Beasts did leap, and birds did sing,
Trees did grow, and plants did spring;
   Everything did banish moan,
   Save the nightingale alone.
Sonnets set to Music, XXI.

Hark, hark! the lark at heaven's gate sings,
   And Phœbus 'gins arise,
His steeds to water at those springs
   On chaliced flowers that lies;
And winking Mary-buds begin
   To ope their golden eyes:
With everything that pretty is,
   My lady sweet, arise, arise.
Cymbeline, Act II. Sc. 3.

When wheat is green, when hawthorn buds appear.
Midsummer Night's Dream, Act I. Sc. I.

May 1.

. . . Take arms against a sea of troubles,
And by opposing end them.
Hamlet, Act III. Sc. 1.

Welcome hither, as is the spring to the earth.
Winter's Tale, Act V. Sc. 1.

May 2.

But what care I for words? Yet words do well
When he that speaks them pleases those that hear.
As You Like It, Act III. Sc. 5.

. . . . I am a man
That from my first have been inclined to thrift.
Timon of Athens, Act I. Sc. 1.

May 3.

She came adorned hither like sweet May.
Richard II. Act V. Sc. 1.

Unquestion'd welcome and undoubted blest.
All's Well that Ends Well, Act II. Sc. 1.

Thou art thy mother's glass, and she in thee
Calls back the lovely April of her prime;
So thou through windows of thine age shalt see
Despite of wrinkles this thy golden time.
Sonnet III.

May 1.

May 2.

May 3.

May 4.

.... This honest creature doubtless
Sees and knows more, much more than he unfolds.

Othello, Act III. Sc. 3.

'Some are born great, some achieve greatness, and some have greatness thrown upon them.'

Twelfth Night, Act V. Sc. 1.

May 5.

Ay, me! for aught that I could ever read,
Could ever hear by tale or history,
The course of true love never did run smooth.

Midsummer Night's Dream, Act I. Sc. 1.

To revenge is no valour, but to bear.

Timon of Athens, Act III. Sc. 5.

May 6.

The elements be kind to thee, and make
Thy spirits all of comfort!

Antony and Cleopatra, Act III. Sc. 2.

How many things by season season'd are
To their right praise and true perfection.

Merchant of Venice, Act V. Sc. 1.

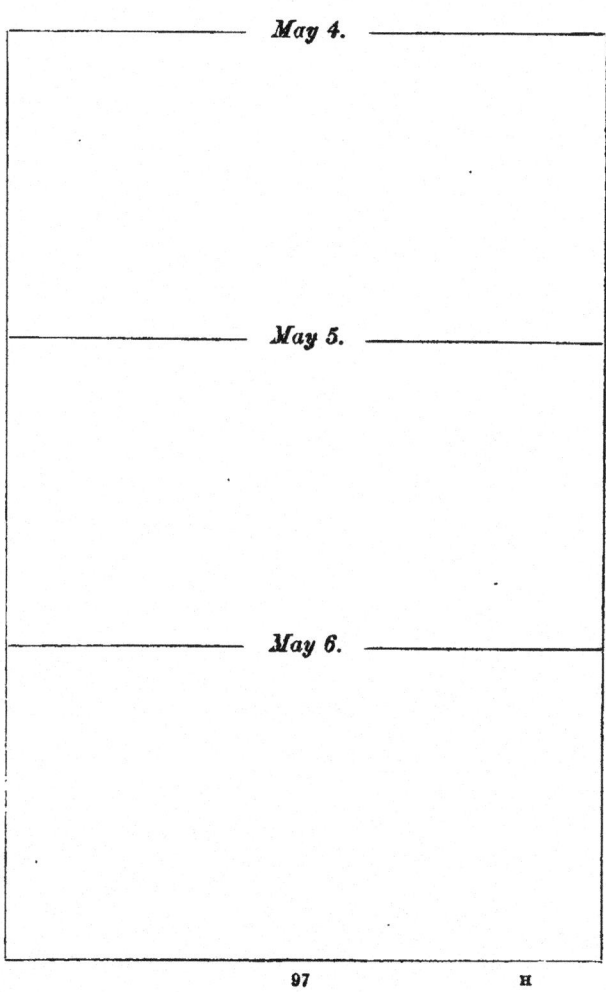

May 4.

May 5.

May 6.

May 7.

The God of heaven
Both now and ever bless her!
Henry VIII. Act V. Sc. 1.

Strong reasons make strong actions.
King John, Act III. Sc. 4.

May 8.

Old fashions please me best; I am not so nice,
To change true rules for old inventions.
Taming of the Shrew, Act III. Sc. 1.

In the world I fill up a place, which may be better supplied when I have made it empty.
As You Like It, Act I. Sc. 2.

May 9.

For what he has he gives, what thinks he shows;
Yet gives he not till judgment guide his bounty.
Troilus and Cressida, Act IV. Sc. 5.

Shall we serve Heaven
With less respect than we do minister
To our gross selves?
Measure for Measure, Act II. Sc. 2.

May 7.

May 8.

May 9.

May 10.

I charge thee, fling away ambition:
By that sin fell the angels; how can man, then,
The image of his Maker, hope to win by it?
Henry VIII. Act III. Sc. 2.

Thou art in a parlous state, shepherd!
As You Like It, Act III. Sc. 2.

May 11.

The good I stand on is my truth and honesty;
. . . . I fear nothing
What can be said against me.
Henry VIII. Act V. Sc. 1.

. . . . . What I can redress,
As I shall find the time to friend, I will.
Macbeth, Act IV. Sc. 3.

May 12.

Would you praise Cæsar, say 'Cæsar: go no further.'
Antony and Cleopatra, Act III. Sc. 2.

Comfort's in heaven; and we are on the earth,
Where nothing lives but crosses, cares and grief.
Richard II. Act II. Sc. 2.

How came we ashore?
By Providence divine.
Tempest, Act I. Sc. 2.

May 10.

May 11.

May 12.

―――― *May 13.* ――――

Trees shall be my books,
And in their barks my thoughts I'll character.
As You Like It, Act III. Sc. 2.

What poor an instrument may do a noble deed!
Antony and Cleopatra, Act V. Sc. 2.

―――― *May 14.* ――――

For never anything can be amiss,
When simpleness and duty tender it.
Midsummer Night's Dream, Act V. Sc. 1.

How green you are, and fresh, in this old world!
King John, Act III. Sc. 4.

―――― *May 15.* ――――

Good fortune guide thee!
Richard III. Act IV. Sc. 1.

Of your philosophy you make no use,
If you give place to accidental evils.
Julius Cæsar, Act IV. Sc. 3.

. . . . Welcome ever smiles,
And farewell goes out sighing.
Troilus and Cressida, Act III. Sc. 3.

———— *May 13.* ————

———— *May 14.* ————

———— *May 15.* ————

―――― *May 16.* ――――

He hath a daily beauty in his life.
Othello, Act V. Sc. 1.

Blessed are the peacemakers on earth.
Second Part of Henry VI. Act II. Sc. 1.

―――― *May 17.* ――――

Love can transpose to form and dignity :
Love looks not with the eyes, but with the mind;
And therefore is wing'd Cupid painted blind.
Midsummer Night's Dream, Act I. Sc. 1.

Thou art as wise as thou art beautiful.
Midsummer Night's Dream, Act III. Sc. 1.

―――― *May 18.* ――――

Like as the waves make towards the pebbled shore,
So do our minutes hasten to their end;
Each changing place with that which goes before,
In sequent toil all forwards do contend.
Sonnet LX.

. . . . No mind that's honest
But in it shares some woe.
Macbeth, Act IV. Sc. 3.

May 16.

May 17.

May 18.

────────── *May 19.* ──────────

I am weary ; yea, my memory is tired.
Coriolanus, Act I. Sc. 9.

The end crowns all,
And that old common arbitrator, Time,
Will one day end it.
Troilus and Cressida, Act IV. Sc. 5.

────────── *May 20.* ──────────

His worth is warrant for his welcome hither.
Two Gentlemen of Verona, Act II. Sc. 4.

An honest tale speeds best being plainly told.
Richard III. Act IV. Sc. 4.

────────── *May 21.* ──────────

Cheer your heart :
Be you not troubled with the time, which drives
O'er your content these strong necessities ;
But let determined things to destiny
Hold unbewailed their way.
Antony and Cleopatra, Act III. Sc. 6.

Were man but constant he were perfect.
Two Gentlemen of Verona, Act V. Sc. 4.

May 19.

May 20.

May 21.

———— May 22. ————

But, O, how bitter a thing it is to look into happiness through another man's eyes!

As You Like It, Act v. Sc. 2.

I must be patient till the heavens look
With an aspect more favourable.

Winter's Tale, Act ii. Sc. 1.

———— May 23. ————

The hand that made you fair hath made you good.

Measure for Measure, Act iii. Sc. 1.

Before the curing of a strong disease,
Even in the instant of repair and health,
The fit is strongest; evils that take leave,
On their departure most of all show evil.

King John, Act iii. Sc. 4.

———— May 24. ————

'God save the Queen.'

Richard III. Act iv. Sc. 4.

The grace of Heaven
Before, behind thee and on every hand,
Enwheel thee round!

Othello, Act ii. Sc. 1.

May 22.

May 23.

May 24.

May 25.

The Lord in heaven bless thee!

Henry V. Act IV. Sc. 1.

A little gale will soon disperse that cloud,
And blow it to the source from whence it came:
The very beams will dry those vapours up,
For every cloud engenders not a storm.

Third Part of Henry VI. Act V. Sc. 3.

May 26.

Fair thoughts be your fair pillow!

Troilus and Cressida, Act III. Sc. 1.

Good angels guard thee!

Richard III. Act IV. Sc. 1.

All I see in you is worthy love.

King John, Act II. Sc. 1.

May 27.

His nature is too noble for the world:
He would not flatter Neptune for his trident,
Or Jove for's power to thunder. His heart's his mouth,
What his breast forges, that his tongue must vent.

Coriolanus, Act III. Sc. 1.

There is no darkness but ignorance.

Twelfth Night, Act IV. Sc. 1.

May 25.

May 26.

May 27.

May 28.

Falseness cannot come from thee.
. . . . thou seem'st a palace
For the crown'd Truth to dwell in.

Pericles, Act V. Sc. 1.

He has my heart yet, and shall have my prayers
While I shall have my life.

Henry VIII. Act III. Sc. 1.

May 29.

Love thyself last.

Henry VIII. Act III. Sc. 2.

God bless thee!

Twelfth Night, Act I. Sc. 5.

My salad days,
When I was green in judgment.

Antony and Cleopatra, Act I. Sc. 5.

May 30.

My project may deceive me,
But my intents are fixed and will not leave me.

All's Well that Ends Well, Act I. Sc. 1.

O, what may man within him hide,
Though angel on the outward side!

Measure for Measure, Act III. Sc. 2.

May 28.

May 29.

May 30.

May 31.

Earth's increase, foison plenty,
Barns and garners never empty,
Vines with clustering bunches growing,
Plants with goodly burthen bowing;
Spring come to you at the farthest
In the very end of harvest!
Scarcity and want shall shun you;
Ceres' blessing so is on you.

Tempest, Act IV. Sc. I.

May 31.

A MIDSUMMER NIGHT'S DREAM.
ACT 2. SCENE 2.

JUNE.

I know a bank where the wild thyme blows,
Where oxlips and the nodding violet grows,
Quite over-canopied with luscious woodbine,
With sweet musk-roses and with eglantine.

Midsummer Night's Dream, Act II. Sc. 1.

Where the bee sucks, there suck I:
In a cowslip's bell I lie;
There I couch when owls do cry.
On a bat's back I do fly
   After summer merrily.
Merrily, merrily shall I live now
Under the blossom that hangs on the bough.

Tempest, Act V. Sc. 1.

June 1.

O 'tis the sun that maketh all things shine.
Love's Labour's Lost, Act IV. Sc. 3.

Out with it boldly, truth loves open dealing.
Henry VIII. Act III. Sc. 1.

June 2.

Rightly to be great
Is not to stir without great argument,
But greatly to find quarrel in a straw
When honour's at the stake.
Hamlet, Act IV. Sc. 4.

A noble life before a long.
Coriolanus, Act III. Sc. 1.

June 3.

But thou art fair, and at thy birth, dear boy,
Nature and Fortune joined to make thee great.
King John, Act III. Sc. 1.

I will be the pattern of all patience: I will say nothing.
King Lear, Act III. Sc. 2.

June 1.

June 2.

June 3.

June 4.

'Tis a lucky day, boy, and we'll do good deeds on't.
Winter's Tale, Act III. Sc. 3.

Pray that the right may thrive.
King Lear, Act v. Sc. 2.

June 5.

And having sworn truth, ever will be true.
Twelfth Night, Act IV. Sc. 3.

. . . . Take a fellow of plain and uncoined constancy, for he perforce must do thee right.
Henry V. Act v. Sc. 2.

June 6.

He robs himself that spends a bootless grief.
Othello, Act I. Sc. 3.

To mourn a mischief that is past and gone
Is the next way to draw new mischief on.
Othello, Act I. Sc. 3.

June 4.

June 5.

June 6.

June 7.

But a good heart, Kate, is the sun and moon; or rather the sun and not the moon; for it shines bright and never changes, but keeps his course truly.

Henry V. Act v. Sc. 2.

He is simply the rarest man i' the world.

Coriolanus, Act IV. Sc. 5.

June 8.

The will of Heaven be done
In this and all things!

Henry VIII. Act I. Sc. 1.

There is a world elsewhere.

Coriolanus, Act III. Sc. 3.

Bliss and goodness on you.

Measure for Measure, Act III. Sc. 2.

June 9.

For miracles are ceased;
And therefore we must needs admit the means
How things are perfected.

Henry V. Act I. Sc. 1.

Polonius. What do you think of me?
King. As of a man faithful and honourable.

Hamlet, Act II. Sc. 2.

June 7.

June 8.

June 9.

June 10.

All the world's a stage,
And all the men and women merely players.
As You Like It, Act II. Sc. 6.

Shall we rest us here,
And by relating tales of others' griefs,
See if 'twill teach us to forget our own?
Pericles, Act I. Sc. 4.

June 11.

Let's further think of this.;
Weigh what convenience both of time and means
May fit us to our shape.
Hamlet, Act IV. Sc. 7.

Striving to better, oft we mar what's well.
King Lear, Act I. Sc. 4.

June 12.

God, the best maker of all marriages,
Combine your hearts in one.
Henry V. Act V. Sc. 2.

Your heart's desires be with you!
As You Like It, Act I. Sc. 2.

A heaven on earth I have won by wooing thee.
All's Well that Ends Well, Act IV. Sc. 1.

June 10.

June 11.

June 12.

―――――― *June 13.* ――――――

Wise men ne'er sit and wail their loss,
But cheerly seek how to redress their harms.
Third Part of Henry VI. Act v. Sc. 4.

Checks and disasters
Grow in the veins of actions highest rear'd.
Troilus and Cressida, Act I. Sc. 3.

―――――― *June 14.* ――――――

I am a man whom fortune hath cruelly scratched.
All's Well that Ends Well, Act v. Sc. 1.

So, on your patience evermore attending,
New joy wait on you!
Pericles, Act v. Sc. 3.

―――――― *June 15.* ――――――

Come what come may,
Time and the hour runs through the roughest day.
Macbeth, Act I. Sc. 3.

Quick is mine ear to hear of good towards him.
Richard II. Act II. Sc. 1.

June 13.

June 14.

June 15.

June 16.

Sweet are the uses of adversity,
Which, like the toad, ugly and venomous,
Wears yet a precious jewel in his head.
As You Like It, Act II. Sc. 1.

. . . . Spirits are not finely touched
But to fine issues.
Measure for Measure, Act I. Sc. 1.

June 17.

Be cheerful; wipe thine eyes:
Some falls are means the happier to arise.
Cymbeline, Act IV. Sc. 2.

The bitter past, more welcome is the sweet.
All's Well that Ends Well, Act V. Sc. 3.

June 18.

Thy truth then be thy dower.
King Lear, Act I. Sc. 1.

You have a nimble wit: I think it was made of Atalanta's heels.
As You Like It, Act III. Sc. 2.

Some Cupid kills with arrows, some with traps.
Much Ado about Nothing, Act III. Sc. 1.

June 16.

June 17.

June 18.

June 19.

Happy in that we are not over-happy.
Hamlet, Act II. Sc. 2.

I do much wonder that one man, seeing how much another man is a fool when he dedicates his behaviours to love, will, after he hath laughed at such shallow follies in others, become the argument of his own scorn by falling in love.
Much Ado about Nothing, Act II. Sc. 3.

June 20.

But I had not so much of man in me,
And all my mother came into my eyes
And gave me up to tears.
Henry V. Act IV. Sc. 6.

The purest treasure mortal times afford
Is spotless reputation.
Richard II. Act I. Sc. 1.

June 21.

Be but duteous, and true preferment shall tender itself to thee.
Cymbeline, Act III. Sc. 5.

Touch you the sourest points with sweetest terms.
Antony and Cleopatra, Act II. Sc. 2.

Happy are they that hear their own detractions, and can put them to mending.
Much Ado about Nothing, Act II. Sc. 3.

June 19.

June 20.

June 21.

―――― *June 22.* ――――

We do pray for mercy ;
And that same prayer doth teach us all to render
The deeds of mercy.
Merchant of Venice, Act IV. Sc. 1.

Men of few words are the best men.
Henry V. Act III. Sc. 2.

―――― *June 23.* ――――

There be many Cæsars
Ere such another Julius.
Cymbeline, Act III. Sc. 1.

Things done well,
And with a care, exempt themselves from fear.
Henry VIII. Act I. Sc. 2.

―――― *June 24.* ――――

And He that doth the ravens feed,
Yea, providently caters for the sparrow,
Be comfort to my age !
As You Like It, Act II. Sc. 3.

As full of spirit as the month of May,
And gorgeous as the sun at midsummer.
First Part of Henry IV. Act IV. Sc. 1.

June 22.

June 23.

June 24.

June 25.

We know what we are, but know not what we may be.
Hamlet, Act IV. Sc. 5.

All that lives must die,
Passing through Nature to eternity.
Hamlet, Act I. Sc. 2.

June 26.

Art thou afeard
To be the same in thine own act and valour
As thou art in desire? . . .
Letting 'I dare not' wait upon 'I would,'
Like the poor cat i' the adage?
Macbeth, Act I. Sc. 7.

Be great in act, as you have been in thought.
King John, Act V. Sc. 1.

June 27.

An honest soul i' faith, Sir, by my troth he is, as ever broke bread.
Much Ado about Nothing, Act III. Sc. 5.

Give sorrow words: the grief that does not speak
Whispers the o'erfraught heart and bids it break.
Macbeth, Act IV. Sc. 3.

June 25.

June 26.

June 27.

June 28.

Shall I compare thee to a summer's day?
Thou art more lovely and more temperate.
Sonnet XVIII.

For 'tis the mind that makes the body rich;
And as the sun breaks through the darkest clouds,
So honour peereth in the meanest habit.
Taming of the Shrew, Act IV. Sc. 3.

June 29.

Mine honour is my life; both grown in one;
Take honour from me, and my life is done.
Richard II. Act I. Sc. 1.

And creep time ne'er so slow,
Yet it shall come for me to do thee good.
King John, Act III. Sc. 3.

June 30.

Be not too tame neither; but let your own discretion be your tutor: suit the action to the word, the word to the action.
Hamlet, Act III. Sc. 2.

Though I am not naturally honest, I am so sometimes by chance.
Winter's Tale, Act IV. Sc. 3.

June 28.

June 29.

June 30.

SHAKESPEARE AND HIS CONTEMPORARIES.

T. DORSET. SAM DANYEL. W. RALEIGH.
W. CAMDEN. F. BACON. J. DENNER. SOUTHAMPTON.
J. SILVESTER. W. BEAUMONT. BEN JONSON. R.C. BRABUR.
J. FLETCHER.
J. GELDRY. T DEKKER

JULY.

FULL many a glorious morning have I seen
Flatter the mountain-tops with sovereign eye,
Kissing with golden face the meadows green,
Gilding pale streams with heavenly alchemy.

Sonnet XXXIII.

Here's flowers for you;
Hot lavender, mints, savory, marjoram;
The marigold, that goes to bed wi' the sun
And with him rises weeping: these are flowers
Of middle summer, and I think they are given
To men of middle age.

Winter's Tale, Act IV. Sc. 4.

July 1.

O, how full of briers is this working-day world!
As You Like It, Act I. Sc. 3.

How far it is
To this same blessed Milford: and by the way
Tell me how Wales was made so happy as
To inherit such a Haven.
Cymbeline, Act III. Sc. 2.

July 2.

'Tis death to me to be at enmity;
I hate it, and desire all good men's love.
Richard III. Act II. Sc. 1.

With thoughts so qualified as your charities shall best instruct you, measure me.
Winter's Tale, Act II. Sc. 1.

July 3.

Muse not that I thus suddenly proceed;
For what I will, I will, and there's an end.
Two Gentlemen of Verona, Act I. Sc. 3.

The love that follows us sometime is our trouble,
Which still we thank as love.
Macbeth, Act I. Sc. 6.

July 1.

July 2.

July 3.

July 4.

A rarer spirit never
Did steer humanity.
>> *Antony and Cleopatra*, Act V. Sc. 1.

I have no other but a woman's reason;
I think him so because I think him so.
>> *Two Gentlemen of Verona*, Act I. Sc. 2.

July 5.

Led on by Heaven, and crown'd with joy at last.
>> *Pericles*, Act V. Sc. 3.

He's truly valiant that can wisely suffer.
>> *Timon of Athens*, Act III. Sc. 5.

July 6.

Down on your knees,
And thank Heaven, fasting, for a good man's love.
>> *As You Like It*, Act III. Sc. 5.

Heaven give you many many merry days.
>> *Merry Wives of Windsor*, Act V. Sc. 5.

An honest man, sir, is able to speak for himself, when a knave is not.
>> *Second Part of Henry IV*. Act V. Sc. 1.

July 4.

July 5.

July 6.

———————— *July 7.* ————————

Love all, trust a few,
Do wrong to none: be able for thine enemy
Rather in power than use, and keep thy friend
Under thy own life's key.
All's Well that Ends Well, Act I. Sc. 1.

Flow,
You heavenly blessings, on her!
Cymbeline, Act III. Sc. 5.

———————— *July 8.* ————————

This day
Shall change all griefs and quarrels into love.
Henry V. Act V. Sc. 2.

I have been troubled in my sleep this night,
But dawning day new comfort hath inspired.
Titus Andronicus, Act II. Sc. 2.

———————— *July 9.* ————————

I wear not motley in my brain.
Twelfth Night, Act V. Sc. 5.

For truth can never be confirmed enough,
Though doubts did ever sleep.
Pericles, Act V. Sc. 1.

July 7.

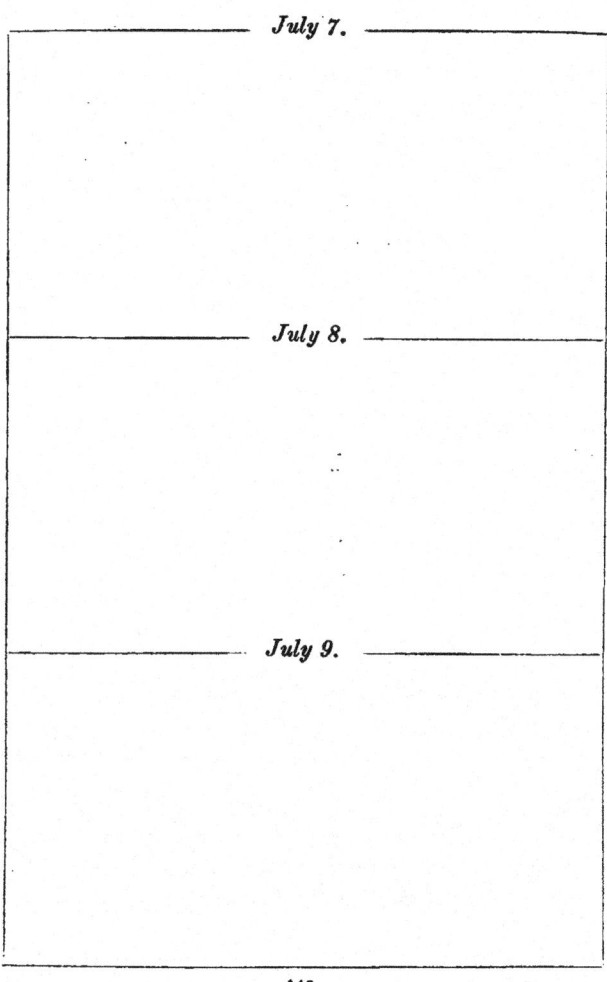

July 8.

July 9.

July 10.

I see men's judgments are
A parcel of their fortunes; and things outward
Do draw the inward quality after them,
To suffer all alike.
Antony and Cleopatra, Act III. Sc. 13.

Be govern'd by your knowledge and proceed
I' the sway of your own will.
King Lear, Act IV. Sc. 7.

July 11.

Truth hath a quiet breast . . . .
For gnarling sorrow hath less power to bite
The man that mocks at it and sets it light.
Richard II. Act I. Sc. 3.

Your face, my thane, is as a book, where men
May read strange matters.
Macbeth, Act I. Sc. 5.

July 12.

The best wishes that can be forged in your thoughts be servants to you!
All's Well that Ends Well, Act I. Sc. 1.

And there at Venice gave
His body to that pleasant country's earth,
And his pure soul unto his Captain Christ,
Under whose colours he had fought so long.
Richard II. Act IV. Sc. 1.

July 10.

July 11.

July 12

─────────── *July 13.* ───────────

One fire burns out another's burning,
One pain is lessen'd by another's anguish.
Romeo and Juliet, Act I. Sc. 2.

For to be wise and love
Exceeds man's might: that dwells with gods above.
Troilus and Cressida, Act III. Sc. 2.

─────────── *July 14.* ───────────

It is not so with Him that all things knows
As 'tis with us that square our guess by shows;
And most it is presumption in us when
The help of Heaven we count the act of men.
All's Well that Ends Well, Act II. Sc. 1.

Nature hath formed strange fellows in her time.
Merchant of Venice, Act I. Sc. 1.

─────────── *July 15.* ───────────

We must take the current when it serves,
Or lose our ventures.
Julius Cæsar, Act IV. Sc. 3.

But men are men; the best sometimes forget.
Othello, Act II. Sc. 3.

Thou dost conspire against thy friend
If thou but think'st him wrong'd, and makest his ear
A stranger to thy thoughts.
Othello, Act III. Sc. 3.

July 13.

July 14.

July 15.

July 16.

True hope is swift, and flies with swallow's wings;
Kings it makes gods, and meaner creatures kings.

Richard III. Act v. Sc. 2.

Mine eyes
Were not in fault, for she was beautiful.

Cymbeline, Act v. Sc. 5.

July 17.

Thou art a summer-bird,
Which ever in the haunch of winter sings
The lifting up of day.

Second Part of Henry IV. Act iv. Sc. 4.

But thy eternal summer shall not fade . . . .
Nor shall Death brag thou wander'st in his shade,
When in eternal lines to time thou growest.

Sonnet xviii.

July 18.

But signs of nobleness, like stars, shall shine
On all deservers.

Macbeth, Act i. Sc. 4.

I do love nothing in the world so well as you:
is not that strange?

Much Ado about Nothing, Act iv. Sc. 1.

July 16.

July 17.

July 18.

―――――― *July 19.* ――――――

　　　　　The blessed gods
Purge all infection from our air whilst you
Do climate here!
　　　　　　　Winter's Tale, Act V. Sc. 1.

He makes a July's day short as December.
　　　　　　　Winter's Tale, Act I. Sc. 2.

―――――― *July 20.* ――――――

We shall try fortune in a second fight.
　　　　　　　Julius Cæsar, Act V. Sc. 3.

I was not born under a rhyming planet, nor I cannot woo in festival terms.
　　　　　　Much Ado about Nothing, Act V. Sc. 2.

―――――― *July 21.* ――――――

　　　　　Thyself and thy belongings
Are not thine own so proper as to waste
Thyself upon thy virtues, they on thee;
Heaven doth with us as we with torches do,
Not light them for themselves; for if our virtues
Did not go forth of us, 'twere all alike
As if we had them not.
　　　　　　Measure for Measure, Act I. Sc 1.

July 19.

July 20.

July 21.

July 22.

There's no art
To find the mind's construction in the face:
He was a gentleman on whom I built
An absolute trust.
Macbeth, Act I. Sc. 4.

Your name, fair gentlewoman?
King Lear, Act I. Sc. 4.

July 23.

The setting sun, and music at the close,
As the last taste of sweets, is sweetest last,
Writ in remembrance more than things long past.
Richard II. Act II. Sc. 1.

Ye speak like honest men; pray God ye prove so!
Henry VIII. Act III. Sc. 1.

July 24.

Prosperity be thy page!
Thy friend no less
Than those she placeth highest!
Coriolanus, Act I. Sc. 5.

He tires betimes that spurs too fast betimes.
Richard II. Act II. Sc. 1.

July 22.

July 23.

July 24.

July 25.

God bless thee, lady!
Twelfth Night, Act I. Sc. 5.

I know you have a gentle, noble temper,
A soul as even as a calm.
Henry VIII. Act III. Sc. 1.

July 26.

I think there's never a man in Christendom
That can less hide his love or hate than he;
For by his face straight shall you know his heart.
Richard III. Act III. Sc. 4.

The sweetest lady that ever I looked on.
Much Ado about Nothing, Act I. Sc. 1.

July 27.

I see some sparks of better hope, which elder years
May happily bring forth.
Richard II. Act V. Sc. 3.

The fire i' the flint shows not till it be struck.
Timon of Athens, Act I. Sc. 1.

July 25.

July 26.

July 27.

July 28.

Her voice was ever soft,
Gentle, and low, an excellent thing in woman.
King Lear, Act v. Sc. 3.

Though thy tackle's torn,
Thou show'st a noble vessel.
Coriolanus, Act iv. Sc. 5.

July 29.

A heart unspotted is not easily daunted.
Second Part of Henry VI. Act iii. Sc. 1.

How still the evening is,
As hush'd on purpose to grace harmony!
Much Ado about Nothing, Act ii. Sc. 3.

God give you quiet rest to-night!
Richard III. Act v. Sc. 3.

July 30.

Our remedies oft in ourselves do lie,
Which we ascribe to Heaven.
All's Well that Ends Well, Act i. Sc. 1.

We are not ourselves
When nature, being oppress'd, commands the mind
To suffer with the body.
King Lear, Act ii. Sc. 4.

July 28.

July 29.

July 30.

July 31.

Wipe not out the rest of thy services by leaving me now: the need I have of thee thine own goodness hath made; better not to have had thee than thus to want thee.
Winter's Tale, Act IV. Sc. 2.

The noblest mind he carries
That ever govern'd man.
Long may he live in fortunes!
Timon of Athens, Act I. Sc. 1.

July 31.

HAMLET.
ACT 3 SCENE 2.

AUGUST.

You sunburnt sickle-men, of August weary,
Come hither from the furrow and be merry:
Make holiday; your rye-straw hats put on,
And these fresh nymphs encounter every one
In country footing.
Tempest, Act IV. Sc. 1.

The year growing ancient,
Not yet on Summer's death, nor on the birth
Of trembling Winter, the fairest flower o' the season
Are our carnations and streak'd gillyvors.
Winter's Tale, Act IV. Sc. 4.

――――――― *August 1.* ―――――――

Haply I think on thee, and then my state,
Like to the lark at break of day arising
From sullen earth, sings hymns at heaven's gate;
For thy sweet love remember'd such wealth brings
That then I scorn to change my state with kings.
Sonnet XXIX.

――――――― *August 2.* ―――――――

Duty never yet did want his meed.
Two Gentlemen of Verona, Act II. Sc. 4.

O, two such silver currents, when they join,
Do glorify the banks that bound them in.
King John, Act II. Sc. 1.

Nothing 'gainst Time's scythe can make defence.
Sonnet XII.

――――――― *August 3.* ―――――――

Bid her have good heart.
Antony and Cleopatra, Act V. Sc. 1.

Then let us teach our trial patience,
Because it is a customary cross.
Midsummer Night's Dream, Act I. Sc. 1.

Past and to come seems best; things present worst.
Second Part of Henry IV. Act I. Sc. 3.

August 1.

August 2.

August 3.

―――― *August 4.* ――――

But Heaven hath a hand in these events,
To whose high will we bound our calm contents.
Richard II. Act v. Sc. 2.

What Heaven more will,
That thee may furnish and my prayers pluck down,
Fall on thy head!
All's Well that Ends Well, Act i. Sc. 1.

―――― *August 5.* ――――

To be merry best becomes you; for, out of question,
you were born in a merry hour.
Much Ado about Nothing, Act ii. Sc. 1.

To business that we love we rise betimes, and go
to't with delight.
Antony and Cleopatra, Act iv. Sc. 4.

―――― *August 6.* ――――

Fortune and Victory sit on thy helm!
Richard III. Act v. Sc. 3.

Hope is a lover's staff; walk hence with that
And manage it against despairing thoughts.
Two Gentlemen of Verona, Act iii. Sc. 1.

. The king-becoming graces,
As justice, verity, temperance, stableness,
Bounty, perseverance, mercy, lowliness,
Devotion, patience, courage, fortitude.
Macbeth, Act iv. Sc. 3.

August 4.

August 5.

August 6.

August 7.

Who is't can say, 'I am at the worst?'
King Lear, Act IV. Sc. I.

Each day still better other's happiness;
Until the heavens, envying earth's good hap,
Add an immortal title to your crown!
Richard II. Act I. Sc. I.

August 8.

You have too much respect upon the world,
They lose it that do buy it with much care.
Merchant of Venice, Act I. Sc. I.

Such duty as the subject owes the prince,
Even such a woman oweth to her husband.
Taming of the Shrew, Act V. Sc. 2.

August 9.

Thrice is he armed that hath his quarrel just.
Second Part of Henry VI. Act III. Sc. 2.

The man that hath no music in himself,
Nor is not moved with concord of sweet sounds,
Is fit for treasons, stratagems, and spoils, . . .
Let no such man be trusted.
Merchant of Venice, Act V. Sc. I.

August 7.

August 8.

August 9.

———————— *August 10.* ————————

Ignorance is the curse of God,
Knowledge the wing wherewith we fly to heaven.
Second Part of Henry VI. Act IV. Sc. 7.

But I thought there was more in him than I could think.
Coriolanus, Act IV. Sc. 5.

———————— *August 11.* ————————

Your fair discourse hath been as sugar,
Making the hard way sweet and delectable.
Richard II. Act II. Sc. 3.

I am as poor as Job, but not so patient.
Second Part of Henry IV. Act I. Sc. 2.

Fast bind, fast find;
A proverb never stale in thrifty mind.
Merchant of Venice, Act II. Sc. 5.

———————— *August 12.* ————————

We will not from the helm to sit and weep,
But keep our course, though the rough wind say no.
Third Part of Henry VI. Act V. Sc. 4.

At all times alike
Men are not still the same: 'twas time and griefs
That framed him thus: time, with his fairer hand,
Offering the fortunes of his former days,
The former man may make him.
Timon of Athens, Act V. Sc. 1.

August 10.

August 11.

August 12.

August 13.

But He, that hath the steerage of my course,
Direct my sail!
Romeo and Juliet, Act I. Sc. 4.

Let all the number of the stars give light
To thy fair way!
Antony and Cleopatra, Act III. Sc. 2.

August 14.

When Fortune means to men most good,
She looks upon them with a threatening eye.
King John, Act III. Sc. 4.

Bright star of Venus fall'n down on the earth,
How may I reverently worship thee enough?
First Part of Henry VI. Act I. Sc. 2.

August 15.

God bless thee; and put meekness in thy mind,
Love, charity, obedience, and true duty!
Richard III. Act II. Sc. 2.

      I hold it cowardice
To rest mistrustful where a noble heart
Hath pawn'd an open hand in sign of love.
Third Part of Henry VI. Act IV. Sc. 2.

August 13.

August 14.

August 15.

─────── *August 16.* ───────

Ah, countryman! if when you make your prayers
God should be so obdurate as yourselves,
How would it fare with your departed souls?
Second Part of Henry VI. Act IV. Sc. 7.

She looks as clear
As morning roses newly washed with dew.
Taming of the Shrew, Act II. Sc. 1.

─────── *August 17.* ───────

The better part of valour is discretion.
First Part of Henry IV. Act V. Sc. 4.

When the sea was calm all boats alike
Show'd mastership in floating.
Coriolanus, Act IV. Sc. 1.

─────── *August 18.* ───────

Take him and use him well, he's worthy of it.
Henry VIII. Act V. Sc. 3.

In the reproof of chance
Lies the true proof of men. . . . Even so
Doth valour's show and valour's worth divide
In storms of fortune.
Troilus and Cressida, Act I. Sc. 3.

August 16.

August 17.

August 18.

August 19.

God be praised, that to believing souls
Gives light in darkness, comfort in despair!
Second Part of Henry VI. Act II. Sc. 1.

Thou hast a perfect thought:
I will upon all hazards well believe
Thou art my friend, that know'st my tongue so well.
King John, Act V. Sc. 6.

August 20.

For 'tis a question left us yet to prove,
Whether love lead fortune, or else fortune love.
Hamlet, Act III. Sc. 2.

For man is a giddy thing, and this is my conclusion.
Much Ado about Nothing, Act V. Sc. 4.

August 21.

A good heart's worth gold.
Second Part of Henry IV. Act II. Sc. 4.

To be a make-peace shall become my age.
Richard II. Act I. Sc. 1.

All have not offended;
For those that were, it is not square to take,
On those that are, revenges: crimes, like lands,
Are not inherited.
Timon of Athens, Act V. Sc. 4.

August 19.

August 20.

August 21.

August 22.

He hath a tear for pity, and a hand
Open as day for melting charity.
Second Part of Henry IV. Act IV. Sc. 4.

Take my blessing: God protect thee!
Into whose hand I give thy life. . . . .
When I am in heaven I shall desire
To see what this child does, and praise my Maker.
Henry VIII. Act V. Sc. 5.

August 23.

But 'tis strange:
And oftentimes, to win us to our harm,
The instruments of darkness tell us truths,
Win us with honest trifles, to betray's
In deepest consequence.
Macbeth, Act I. Sc. 3.

Look, he's winding up the watch of his wit; by and by it will strike.
Tempest, Act II. Sc. 1.

August 24.

Is not birth, beauty, good shape, discourse, manhood, learning, gentleness, virtue, youth, liberality, and such-like, the spice and salt that season a man?
Troilus and Cressida, Act I. Sc. 2.

The empty vessel makes the greatest sound.
Henry V. Act IV. Sc. 4.

August 22.

August 23.

August 24.

August 25.

He that of greatest works is finisher,
Oft does them by the weakest minister.
All's Well that Ends Well, Act II. Sc. 1.

Win straying souls . . . .
Cast none away.
Henry VIII. Act v. Sc. 3.

August 26.

A kind heart he hath.
Merry Wives of Windsor, Act III. Sc. 4.

Wherever the bright sun of heaven shall shine,
His honour, and the greatness of his name shall be.
Henry VIII. Act v. Sc. 5.

Is she not passing fair?
Two Gentlemen of Verona, Act IV. Sc. 4.

August 27.

Fair be all thy hopes,
And prosperous be thy life in peace and war!
First Part of Henry VI. Act II. Sc. 5.

Then speak the truth by her; if not divine,
Yet let her be a principality,
Sovereign to all the creatures on the earth.
Two Gentlemen of Verona, Act II. Sc. 4.

August 25.

August 26.

August 27.

--- *August 28.* ---

Think of me as you please.
Twelfth Night, Act v. Sc. 1.

Therefore was I created with a stubborn outside, with an aspect of iron.
Henry V. Act v. Sc. 2.

The strawberry grows underneath the nettle.
Henry V. Act I. Sc. 1.

--- *August 29.* ---

Methinks there is much reason in his sayings.
Julius Cæsar, Act III. Sc. 2.

Forbear to judge, for we are sinners all.
Second Part of Henry VI. Act III. Sc. 3.

Every one can master a grief but he that has it.
Much Ado about Nothing, Act III. Sc. 2.

--- *August 30.* ---

The quality of mercy is not strain'd.
It droppeth as the gentle rain from heaven
Upon the place beneath: it is twice blest;
It blesseth him that gives and him that takes.
Merchant of Venice, Act IV. Sc. 1.

Will Fortune never come with both hands full?
Second Part of Henry IV. Act IV. Sc. 4.

August 28.

August 29.

August 30.

August 31.

There's nothing ill can dwell in such a temple.
If the ill spirit have so fair a house,
Good things will strive to dwell with 't.
Tempest, Act I. Sc. 2.

He is the half part of a blessed man,
Left to be finished by such as she;
And she a fair divided excellence,
Whose fulness of perfection lies in him.
King John, Act II. Sc. 1.

August 31.

KING HENRY, VIII.
ACT 2. SCENE 4.

SEPTEMBER.

ROUGH winds do shake the darling buds of May,
And Summer's lease hath all too short a date :
Sometime too hot the eye of heaven shines,
And often is his gold complexion dimm'd ;
And every fair from fair sometime declines,
By chance or nature's changing course untrimm'd.
Sonnet XVIII.

Not that the Summer is less pleasant now
Than when her mournful hymns did hush the night,
But that wild music burthens every bough,
And sweets grown common lose their dear delight.
Sonnet CII.

September 1.

The strong necessity of time commands
Our services awhile; but my full heart
Remains in use with you.

Antony and Cleopatra, Act I. Sc. 3.

Is it possible he should know what he is and be that he is?

All's Well that Ends Well, Act IV. Sc. 1.

September 2.

The time is worth the use on't.

Winter's Tale, Act III. Sc. 1.

I come not, friends, to steal away your hearts:
I am no orator, as Brutus is;
But, as you know me all, a plain blunt man, . . .
For I have neither wit, nor words, nor worth,
Action, nor utterance, nor the power of speech,
To stir men's blood: I only speak right on.

Julius Cæsar, Act III. Sc. 2.

September 3.

To thee and thy company I bid
A hearty welcome.

Tempest, Act V. Sc. 1.

Confess yourself to Heaven.
Repent what's past: avoid what is to come.

Hamlet, Act III. Sc. 4.

Truly, I would the gods had made thee poetical.

As You Like It, Act III. Sc. 3.

September 1.

September 2.

September 3.

September 4.

We will not stand to prate;
Talkers are no good doers: be assured
We come to use our hands and not our tongues.
Richard III. Act I. Sc. 3.

But, in the verity of extolment,
I take him to be a soul of great article.
Hamlet, Act V. Sc. 2.

September 5.

You were born under a charitable star.
All's Well that Ends Well, Act I. Sc. 1.

O mickle is the powerful grace that lies
In herbs, plants, stones, and their true qualities.
Romeo and Juliet, Act II. Sc. 3.

September 6.

She is a gallant creature, and complete
In mind and feature.
Henry VIII. Act III. Sc. 2.

A proper man as one shall see in a summer's day.
Midsummer Night's Dream, Act I. Sc. 2.

My words fly up, my thoughts remain below.
Words without thoughts never to Heaven go.
Hamlet, Act III. Sc. 3.

September 4.

September 5.

September 6.

September 7.

Whate'er it be, be thou still like thyself,
And sit thee by our side : yield not thy neck
To fortune's yoke, but let thy dauntless mind
Still ride in triumph over all mischance.
Third Part of Henry VI. Act III. Sc. 3.

What stronger breastplate than a heart untainted?
Second Part of Henry VI. Act III. Sc. 2.

September 8.

Whose star-like nobleness gave life and influence
To their whole being!
Timon of Athens, Act V. Sc. 1.

In maiden meditation fancy free.
Midsummer Night's Dream, Act II. Sc. 1.

September 9.

Happy is your Grace,
That can translate the stubbornness of fortune
Into so quiet and so sweet a style.
As You Like It, Act II. Sc. 1.

O most delicate fiend!
Who is't can read a woman?
Cymbeline, Act V. Sc. 5.

September 7.

September 8.

September 9.

September 10.

I am sure care's an enemy to life.
Twelfth Night, Act I. Sc. 3.

Be merry; you have cause,
So have we all, of joy; for our escape
Is much beyond our loss. . . . .
Then wisely weigh
Our sorrow with our comfort.
Tempest, Act II. Sc. 1.

September 11.

Words are easy, like the wind;
Faithful friends are hard to find.
Sundry Sonnets, XXI.

Small cheer and great welcome make a merry feast.
Comedy of Errors, Act III. Sc. 1.

September 12.

He is as full of valour as of kindness.
Henry V. Act IV. Sc. 3.

. . . . My way of life
Is fall'n into the sear, the yellow leaf.
Macbeth, Act V. Sc. 3.

Fate, show thy force: ourselves we do not owe;
What is decreed must be, and be this so.
Twelfth Night, Act I. Sc. 5.

September 10.

September 11.

September 12.

September 13.

She that was ever fair and never proud,
Had tongue at will, and yet was never loud,
Never lack'd gold, and yet went never gay, . . .
She that being anger'd, her revenge being nigh,
Bade her wrong stay, and her displeasure fly.
Othello, Act II. Sc. 1.

A good man's fortune may grow out at heels.
King Lear, Act II. Sc. 2.

September 14.

Charmian. Good sir, give me good fortune.
Soothsayer. I make not, but foresee.
Char. Pray, then, foresee me one.
Antony and Cleopatra, Act I. Sc. 2.

Hast any philosophy in thee, shepherd?
As You Like It, Act III. Sc. 2.

September 15.

Thy tender-hefted nature shall not give
Thee o'er to harshness.
King Lear, Act II. Sc. 4.

When remedies are past, the griefs are ended
By seeing the worst, which late on hopes depended.
Othello, Act I. Sc. 3.

Alack, when once our grace we have forgot,
Nothing goes right: we would, and we would not.
Measure for Measure, Act IV. Sc. 4.

September 13.

September 14.

September 15.

―――― *September 16.* ――――

I am ashamed that women are so simple
To offer war where they should kneel for peace;
Or seek for rule, supremacy, and sway,
When they are bound to serve, love, and obey.
Taming of the Shrew, Act V. Sc. 2.

Do you not think he thinks himself a better man than I am? *Troilus and Cressida*, Act II. Sc. 3.

―――― *September 17.* ――――

I'll note you in my book of memory.
First Part of Henry VI. Act II. Sc. 4.

The spirit of the time shall teach me speed.
King John, Act IV. Sc. 2.

―――― *September 18.* ――――

I am not merry; but I do beguile
The thing I am, by seeming otherwise.
Othello, Act II. Sc. 1.

I am a man
More sinn'd against than sinning.
King Lear, Act III. Sc. 2.

But nature never framed a woman's heart
Of prouder stuff than that of Beatrice.
Much Ado about Nothing, Act III. Sc. 1.

September 16.

September 17.

September 18.

―――― *September 19.* ――――

I have bought
Golden opinions from all sorts of people, . . .
I dare do all that may become a man;
Who dares do more is none.
Macbeth, Act I. Sc. 7.

The sullen passage of thy weary steps
Esteem as foil wherein thou art to set
The precious jewel of thy home return.
Richard II. Act I. Sc. 3.

―――― *September 20.* ――――

The report of her is extended more than can be thought to begin from such a cottage.
Winter's Tale, Act IV. Sc. 2.

He that is thy friend indeed,
He will help thee in thy need.
Sundry Sonnets, XXI.

―――― *September 21.* ――――

Here's metal more attractive.
Hamlet, Act III. Sc. 2.

I am the very pink of courtesy.
Romeo and Juliet, Act II. Sc. 4.

The earth hath bubbles, as the water has,
And these are of them.
Macbeth, Act I. Sc. 3.

Stop up the access and passage to remorse.
Macbeth, Act I. Sc. 5.

September 19.

September 20.

September 21.

September 22.

'Tis in ourselves that we are thus or thus. Our bodies are our gardens, to the which our wills are gardeners; so that if we will plant nettles, or sow lettuce, set hyssop and weed up thyme, . . . have it sterile with idleness, or manured with industry, why, the power and corrigible authority of this lies in our wills.
Othello, Act I. Sc. 3.

September 23.

His life was gentle, and the elements
So mix'd in him, that Nature might stand up
And say to all the world, 'This was a man!'
Julius Cæsar, Act v. Sc. 5.

She bore a mind that envy could not but call fair.
Twelfth Night, Act II. Sc. 1.

September 24.

Is she kind as she is fair?
For beauty lives with kindness.
Love doth to her eyes repair,
To help him of his blindness,
And, being help'd, inhabits there.
Two Gentlemen of Verona, Act IV. Sc. 1.

I to the world am like a drop of water,
That in the ocean seeks another drop.
Comedy of Errors, Act I. Sc. 2.

September 22.

September 23.

September 24.

September 25.

He hath a heart as sound as a bell, and his tongue is the clapper; for what his heart thinks his tongue speaks.
Much Ado about Nothing, Act III. Sc. 2.

Sir, as I have a soul, she is an angel.
Henry VIII. Act IV. Sc. 1.

September 26.

I do believe you think what now you speak;
But what we do determine oft we break.
Hamlet, Act III. Sc. 2.

We bring forth weeds
When our quick minds lie still.
Antony and Cleopatra, Act I. Sc. 2.

Self-love, my liege, is not so vile a sin
As self-neglecting. *Henry V.* Act II. Sc. 4.

September 27.

The clock upbraids me with the waste of time.
Twelfth Night, Act III. Sc. 1.

The time of life is short!
To spend that shortness basely were too long,
If life did ride upon a dial's point,
Still ending at the arrival of an hour.
First Part of Henry IV. Act V. Sc. 2.

September 25.

September 26.

September 27.

September 28.

My gentle lady,
I wish you all the joy that you can wish.
Merchant of Venice, Act III. Sc. 2.

O, while you live, tell truth and shame the devil.
First Part of Henry IV. Act III. Sc. 1.

September 29.

For a light heart lives long.
Love's Labour's Lost, Act V. Sc. 2.

When I said I would die a bachelor, I did not think I should live till I were married.
Much Ado about Nothing, Act II. Sc. 3.

September 30.

Friendship is constant in all other things
Save in the office and affairs of love:
Therefore all hearts in love use their own tongues;
Let every eye negotiate for itself,
And trust no agent.
Much Ado about Nothing, Act II. Sc. 1.

Jesters do oft prove prophets.
King Lear, Act V. Sc. 3.

September 28.

September 29.

September 30.

MERCHANT OF VENICE.
ACT 3. SCENE 2

OCTOBER.

I BEHOLD the violet past prime,
And sable curls all silver'd o'er with white;
When lofty trees I see barren of leaves,
Which erst from heat did canopy the herd,
And Summer's green all girded up in sheaves,
Borne on the bier with white and bristly beard.
Sonnet XII.

How sweet the moonlight sleeps upon this bank!
Here will we sit and let the sounds of music
Creep in our ears: soft stillness and the night
Become the touches of sweet harmony.
Merchant of Venice, Act V. Sc. 1.

As brown in hue
As hazel-nuts, and sweeter than the kernels.
Taming of the Shrew, Act II. Sc. 1.

October 1.

It is the witness still of excellency
To put a strange face on his own perfection.
Much Ado about Nothing, Act II. Sc. 3.

The air of Paradise did fan the house,
And angels officed all.
All's Well that Ends Well, Act III. Sc. 2.

October 2.

Here is a dear, a true industrious friend.
First Part of Henry IV. Act I. Sc. 1.

And but he's something stained with grief (that's beauty's canker), thou might'st call him a goodly person.
Tempest, Act I. Sc. 2.

October 3.

Strike now, or else the iron cools.
Third Part of Henry VI. Act V. Sc. 1.

God made him, and therefore let him pass for a man.
Merchant of Venice, Act I. Sc. 2.

Do you not know I am a woman? When I think, I must speak.
As You Like It, Act III. Sc. 2.

October 1.

October 2.

October 3.

October 4.

Beware of entrance to a quarrel, but being in,
Bear't that the opposed may beware of thee.
Hamlet, Act I. Sc. 3.

Do as adversaries do in law,
Strive mightily, but eat and drink as friends.
Taming of the Shrew, Act I. Sc. 2.

October 5.

Give every man thine ear, but few thy voice;
Take each man's censure, but reserve thy judgment.
Hamlet, Act I. Sc. 3.

Octavia is of a holy, cold, and still conversation.
Antony and Cleopatra, Act II. Sc. 6.

October 6.

Love is an ever-fixed mark,
That looks on tempests and is never shaken;
It is the star to every wandering bark,
Whose worth's unknown, although his height be taken.
Sonnet CXVI.

When sorrows come they come not single spies,
But in battalions.
Hamlet, Act IV. Sc. 5.

October 4.

October 5.

October 6.

October 7.

God in thy good cause make thee prosperous!
Richard II. Act I. Sc. 3.

If I do vow a friendship, I'll perform it
To the last article.
Othello, Act III. Sc. 3.

October 8.

How sour sweet music is
When time is broke and no proportion kept!
So is it in the music of men's lives.
Richard II. Act V. Sc. 5.

Life every man holds dear; but the brave man
Holds honour far more precious dear than life.
Troilus and Cressida, Act V. Sc. 3.

October 9.

Till now I never knew thee!
Henry VIII. Act I. Sc. 4.

Things without all remedy
Should be without regard; what's done is done.
Macbeth, Act III. Sc. 2.

A son who is the theme of honour's tongue,
Amongst a grove the very straightest plant.
First Part of Henry IV. Act I. Sc. 1.

October 7.

October 8.

October 9.

―――――― *October 10.* ――――――

All this day an unaccustomed spirit
Lifts me above the ground with cheerful thoughts.
Romeo and Juliet, Act V. Sc. 1.

The smallest worm will turn being trodden on.
Third Part of Henry VI. Act II. Sc. 2.

―――――― *October 11.* ――――――

Fortune brings in some boats that are not steer'd.
Cymbeline, Act IV. Sc. 3.

Let us rather
Hold fast the mortal sword, and like good men
Bestride our downfall'n birthdom.
Macbeth, Act IV. Sc. 3.

―――――― *October 12.* ――――――

Heaven give your spirits comfort.
Measure for Measure, Act IV. Sc. 2.

There is a history in all men's lives,
Figuring the nature of the time deceased;
The which observed, a man may prophesy,
With a near aim, of the main chance of things
As yet not come to life, which in their seeds
And weak beginnings lie intreasured.
Second Part of Henry IV. Act III. Sc. 1.

October 10.

October 11.

October 12.

―――― *October 13.* ――――

I had rather seal my lips, than, to my peril,
Speak that which is not.
Antony and Cleopatra, Act V. Sc. 2.

I'll make assurance doubly sure.
And take a bond of fate,
Macbeth, Act IV. Sc. 1.

―――― *October 14.* ――――

May the gods direct you to the best!
Cymbeline, Act III. Sc. 4.

Well, I know not
What counts harsh fortune casts upon my face:
But in my bosom shall she never come,
To make my heart her vassal.
Antony and Cleopatra, Act II. Sc. 6.

―――― *October 15.* ――――

However God or fortune cast my lot,
There lives or dies,
A loyal, just, and upright gentleman.
Richard II. Act I. Sc. 3.

Age cannot wither her, nor custom stale
Her infinite variety. *Antony and Cleopatra,* Act II. Sc. 2.

. . . . Honours thrive,
When rather from our acts we them derive
Than our foregoers.
All's Well that Ends Well, Act II. Sc. 3.

October 13.

October 14.

October 15.

———— *October 16.* ————

Fie, foh, and fum,
I smell the blood of a British man.
King Lear, Act III. Sc. 4.

Our doubts are traitors,
And make us lose the good we oft might win
By fearing to attempt.
Measure for Measure, Act I. Sc. 4.

Bliss be upon you!
Romeo and Juliet, Act V. Sc. 3.

———— *October 17.* ————

His overthrow heap'd happiness upon him;
For then, and not till then, he felt himself,
And found the blessedness of being little.
Henry VIII. Act IV. Sc. 2.

Here's one, a friend, and one that knows you well.
Romeo and Juliet, Act V. Sc. 3.

———— *October 18.* ————

Our fortune lies upon this jump.
Antony and Cleopatra, Act III. Sc. 8.

My desolation does begin to make
A better life.
Antony and Cleopatra, Act V. Sc. 2.

There is a kind of character in thy life,
That to the observer doth thy history
Fully unfold.
Measure for Measure, Act I. Sc. 1.

October 16.

October 17.

October 18.

───────── *October 19.* ─────────

We are in God's hand, brother.
Henry V. Act III. Sc. 6.

But wonder on, till truth make all things plain.
Midsummer Night's Dream, Act V. Sc. 1.

───────── *October 20.* ─────────

The benediction of these covering heavens
Fall on their heads like dew!
Cymbeline, Act V. Sc. 5.

What thou would'st highly,
That would'st thou holily; would'st not play false.
Macbeth, Act I. Sc. 5.

───────── *October 21.* ─────────

There is a tide in the affairs of men,
Which, taken at the flood, leads on to fortune;
Omitted, all the voyage of their life
Is bound in shallows and in miseries.
Julius Cæsar, Act IV. Sc. 3.

He was my friend, faithful and just to me.
Julius Cæsar, Act III. Sc. 2.

October 19.

October 20.

October 21.

October 22.

A most poor man, made tame by fortune's blows.
King Lear, Act IV. Sc. 6.

Keep your fellows' counsels and your own.
Much Ado about Nothing, Act III. Sc. 3.

October 23.

Nought's had, all's spent
Where our desire is got without content:
'Tis safer to be that which we destroy
Than by destruction dwell in doubtful joy.
Macbeth, Act III. Sc. 2.

I will hope
Of better deeds to-morrow. Rest you happy!
Antony and Cleopatra, Act I. Sc. I.

October 24.

The force of his own merit makes his way.
Henry VIII. Act I. Sc. I.

That old and antique song we heard last night:
Methought it did relieve my passion much,
More than light air and recollected terms
Of these most brisk and giddy-paced times.
Twelfth Night, Act II. Sc. 4.

October 22.

October 23.

October 24.

―――― *October 25.* ――――

So every bondman in his own hand bears
The power to cancel his captivity.
Julius Cæsar, Act I. Sc. 3.

Tut, tut,
Thou troublest me ; I am not in the vein.
Richard III. Act IV. Sc. 2.

―――― *October 26.* ――――

I do not think a braver gentleman,
More active-valiant, or more valiant-young,
More daring or more bold, is now alive
To grace this latter age with noble deeds.
First Part of Henry IV. Act V. Sc. 1.

Great floods have flown from simple sources.
All's Well that Ends Well, Act II. Sc. 1.

―――― *October 27.* ――――

Many years of happy days befall.
Romeo and Juliet, Act I. Sc. 1.

. . . . Who is so full of grace
That it flows over on all that need.
Antony and Cleopatra, Act V. Sc. 2.

But this all lies within the will of God,
To whom I do appeal.
Henry V. Act I. Sc. 2.

October 25.

October 26.

October 27.

October 28.

Then, Heaven, set ope thy everlasting gates,
To entertain my vows of thanks and praise!
Second Part of Henry VI. Act IV. Sc. 9.

He wears his faith but as the fashion of his hat; it ever changes with the next block.
Much Ado about Nothing, Act I. Sc. 1.

October 29.

I count myself in nothing else so happy
As in a soul remembering my good friends.
Richard II. Act II. Sc. 3.

I weigh my friend's affection with mine own.
Timon of Athens, Act I. Sc. 2.

October 30.

Chi non ti vede, non ti pretia.
Love's Labour's Lost, Act IV. Sc. 2.

His words are bonds, his oaths are oracles,
His love sincere, his thoughts immaculate,
His tears pure messengers sent from his heart,
His heart as far from fraud as heaven from earth.
Two Gentlemen of Verona, Act II. Sc. 7.

I cannot but remember such things were,
That were most precious to me.
Macbeth, Act IV. Sc. 3.

October 28.

October 29.

October 30.

October 31.

('HALLOW E'EN.')

To be, or not to be: that is the question.
Hamlet, Act III. Sc. 1.

Thy own wish, wish I thee in every place!
Love's Labour's Lost, Act II. Sc. 1.

Though fortune's malice overthrow my state,
My mind exceeds the compass of her wheel.
Third Part of Henry VI. Act IV. Sc. 3.

October 31.

OTHELLO.
ACT I SCENE 3

NOVEMBER.

With hey, ho, the wind and the rain,—
Must make content with his fortunes fit,
For the rain it raineth every day.

King Lear, Act III. Sc. 2.

The very birds are mute;
Or, if they sing, 'tis with so dull a cheer
That leaves look pale, dreading the winter's near.

Sonnet XCVII.

November 1.

Then God forgive the sin of all those souls
That to their everlasting residence,
Before the dew of evening fall, shall fleet.
King John, Act II. Sc. 1.

For some must watch, while some must sleep :
So runs the world away.
Hamlet, Act III. Sc. 2.

November 2.

Thou hast mettle enough in thee to kill care.
Much Ado about Nothing, Act V. Sc. 1.

Deep malice makes too deep incision.
Forget, forgive, conclude and be agreed.
Richard II. Act I. Sc. 1.

All that glisters is not gold.
Merchant of Venice, Act II. Sc. 7.

November 3.

My heart is great; but it must break with silence,
Ere 't be disburden'd with a liberal tongue.
Richard II. Act II. Sc. 1.

You taught me how to know the face of right.
King John, Act V. Sc. 2.

'Tis beauty that doth oft make woman proud;
'Tis virtue that doth make them most admired;
'Tis government that makes them seem divine.
Third Part of Henry VI. Act I. Sc. 4.

November 1.

November 2.

November 3.

November 4.

For I know thou'rt full of love and honesty,
And weigh'st thy words before thou givest them breath.
Othello, Act III. Sc. 3.

Make of your prayers one sweet sacrifice,
And lift my soul to heaven.
Henry VIII. Act II. Sc. 1.

November 5.

My endeavours
Have ever come too short of my desires.
Henry VIII. Act III. Sc. 2.

For the man doth fear God, howsoever it seems
not in him by some large jests he will make.
Much Ado about Nothing, Act II. Sc. 3.

November 6.

We cannot weigh our brother with ourself.
Measure for Measure, Act II. Sc. 2.

This must my comfort be,
That sun that warms you here shall shine on me.
Richard II. Act I. Sc. 3.

I am a fellow o' the strangest mind i' the world.
Twelfth Night, Act I. Sc. 3.

November 4.

November 5.

November 6.

―――― *November 7.* ――――

Her that loves him with that excellence
That angels love good men with.
Henry VIII. Act II. Sc. 2.

If wishes would prevail with me,
My purpose should not fail with me.
Henry V. Act III. Sc. 2.

―――― *November 8.* ――――

He is complete in feature and in mind,
With all good grace to grace a gentleman.
Two Gentlemen of Verona, Act II. Sc. 1.

But my prayers
For ever and for ever shall be yours.
Henry VIII. Act III. Sc. 2.

―――― *November 9.* ――――

All the gods go with you! upon your sword
Sit laurel victory! and smooth success
Be strew'd before your feet!
Antony and Cleopatra, Act I. Sc. 3.

Nought shall make us rue,
If England to itself do rest but true.
King John, Act V. Sc. 7.

November 7.

November 8.

November 9.

―――― *November 10.* ――――

But men may construe things after their fashion,
Clean from the purpose of the things themselves.
Julius Cæsar, Act I. Sc. 3.

And oft 'tis seen, the wicked prize itself
Buys out the law : but 'tis not so above :
There is no shuffling ; there the action lies
In his true nature ; and we ourselves compell'd,
Even to the teeth and forehead of our faults,
To give in evidence. What then? what rests ?
Try what repentance can. *Hamlet*, Act III. Sc. 3.

―――― *November 11.* ――――

Direct not him whose way himself will choose :
'Tis breath thou lack'st, and that breath wilt thou lose.
Richard II. Act II. Sc. 1.

Give me that man
That is not passion's slave, and I will wear him
In my heart's core, ay, in my heart of heart,
As I do thee. *Hamlet*, Act III. Sc. 2.

―――― *November 12.* ――――

Model to thy inward greatness,
Like little body with a mighty heart.
Henry V. Act II. Chorus.

For courage mounteth with occasion.
King John, Act II. Sc. 1.

And for this once my will shall stand for law.
Third Part of Henry VI. Act IV. Sc. 1.

November 10.

November 11.

November 12.

―――――― *November 13.* ――――――

What a piece of work is a man! How noble in reason! how infinite in faculty! in form and moving, how express and admirable! in action, how like an angel! in apprehension, how like a god! the beauty of the world! the paragon of animals!
Hamlet, Act II. Sc. 2.

Men should be what they seem.
Othello, Act III. Sc. 3.

―――――― *November 14.* ――――――

Things at the worst will cease.
Macbeth, Act IV. Sc. 2.

For there was never yet philosopher
That could endure the toothache patiently,
However they have writ the style of gods
And made a push at chance and sufferance.
Much Ado about Nothing, Act V. Sc. 1.

―――――― *November 15.* ――――――

The dews of heaven fall thick in blessings on her!
Henry VIII. Act IV. Sc. 2.

        O, it is excellent
To have a giant's strength; but it is tyrannous
To use it like a giant.
Measure for Measure, Act II. Sc. 2.

    . . . . I might not this believe
Without the sensible and true avouch
Of mine own eyes. *Hamlet*, Act I. Sc. 1.

November 13.

November 14.

November 15.

November 16.

He cannot flatter, he,
An honest mind and plain, he must speak truth!
An they will take it, so; if not, he's plain.
King Lear, Act II. Sc. 2.

You bear a gentle mind, and heavenly blessings
Follow such creatures.
Henry VIII. Act II. Sc. 3.

November 17.

God's goodness hath been great to thee:
Let never day nor night unhallow'd pass,
But still remember what the Lord hath done.
Second Part of Henry VI. Act II. Sc. 1.

God send every one their heart's desire.
Much Ado about Nothing, Act III. Sc. 4.

November 18.

Be checked for silence, but never taxed for speech.
All's Well that Ends Well, Act I. Sc. 1.

My ending is despair,
Unless I be relieved by prayer,
Which pierces so that it assaults
Mercy itself, and frees all faults.
Tempest, Epil.

God comfort him in this necessity!
First Part of Henry VI. Act IV. Sc. 3.

November 16.

November 17.

November 18.

———— *November 19.* ————

Let me put in your minds, if you forget,
What you have been ere now, and what you are.
Richard III. Act I. Sc. 3.

I forgive and quite forget old faults.
Third Part of Henry VI. Act III. Sc. 3.

She loved me for the dangers I had pass'd,
And I loved her that she did pity them.
Othello, Act I. Sc. 3.

———— *November 20.* ————

Our indiscretion sometimes serves us well,
When our deep plots do pall: and that should teach us
There's a divinity that shapes our ends,
Rough-hew them how we will. *Hamlet,* Act V. Sc. 2.

I have heard you say
That we shall see and know our friends in heaven:
If that be true, I shall see my boy again.
King John, Act III. Sc. 4.

———— *November 21.* ————

Now the fair goddess, Fortune,
Fall deep in love with thee; and her great charms
Misguide thy opposers' swords!
Coriolanus, Act I. Sc. 5.

And tell me now, sweet friend, what happy gale
Blows you to Padua here from old Verona?
Such wind as scatters young men through the world,
To seek their fortunes farther than at home,
Where small experience grows.
Taming of the Shrew, Act I. Sc. 2.

November 19.

November 20.

November 21.

November 22.

It is religion that doth make vows kept.
King John, Act III. Sc. 1.

Our rash faults
Make trivial price of serious things we have,
Not knowing them until we know their grave.
All's Well that Ends Well, Act v. Sc. 3.

November 23.

To show the world I am a gentleman.
Richard II. Act III. Sc. 1.

Good name in man and woman, dear my lord,
Is the immediate jewel of their souls: . . .
Poor and content is rich and rich enough,
But riches fineless is as poor as winter
To him that ever fears he shall be poor.
Othello, Act III. Sc. 3.

November 24.

Sudden sorrow
Serves to say thus, some good thing comes to-morrow.
Second Part of Henry IV. Act IV. Sc. 2.

Mine honesty
Shall not make poor my greatness, nor my power
Work without it.
Antony and Cleopatra, Act II. Sc. 2.

November 22.

November 23.

November 24.

November 25.

Let's take the instant by the forward top;
For we are old, and on our quick'st decrees
The inaudible and noiseless foot of Time
Steals ere we can effect them.
All's Well that Ends Well, Act v. Sc. 3.

Bosom up my counsel, you'll find it wholesome.
Henry VIII. Act I. Sc. I.

November 26.

There is no time so miserable but a man may be true.
Timon of Athens, Act IV. Sc. 3.

To climb steep hills requires slow pace at first.
Henry VIII. Act I. Sc. I.

November 27.

Now, good angels
Fly o'er thy royal head, and shade thy person
Under their blessed wings!
Henry VIII. Act v. Sc. I.

Full of noble device, of all sorts enchantingly beloved.
As You Like It, Act I. Sc. I.

November 25.

November 26.

November 27.

November 28.

My man's as true as steel.
Romeo and Juliet, Act II. Sc. 4.

Our separation so abides, and flies,
That thou, residing here, go'st yet with me,
And I, hence fleeting, here remain with thee.
Antony and Cleopatra, Act I. Sc. 3.

November 29.

I'll take thy word for faith, not ask thine oath:
Who shuns not to break one will sure crack both.
Pericles, Act I. Sc. 2.

They say miracles are past; and we have our philosophical persons, to make modern and familiar things supernatural and causeless.
All's Well that Ends Well, Act II. Sc. 3.

November 30.

('ST. ANDREW'S DAY.')

As heart can think: there is not such a word
Spoke of in Scotland as this term of fear.
First Part of Henry IV. Act IV. Sc. 1.

Remember thee! Ay, while memory holds
A seat in this distracted globe.
Hamlet, Act I. Sc. 4.

My caution was more pertinent
Than the rebuke you give it.
Coriolanus, Act II. Sc. 2.

November 28.

November 29.

November 30.

KING LEAR.
ACT 3 SCENE 2

DECEMBER.

THAT time of year thou may'st in me behold
When yellow leaves, or none, or few, do hang
Upon those boughs which shake against the cold,
Bare ruin'd choirs, where late the sweet birds sang.

Sonnet LXXIII.

What should we speak of
. . . . . . when we shall hear
The rain and wind beat dark December? how,
In this our pinching cave, shall we discourse
The freezing hours away?

Cymbeline, Act III. Sc. 3.

December 1.

Came of a gentle, kind, and noble stock.
Pericles, Act V. Sc. 1.

Her peerless feature, joined with her birth,
Approves her fit for none but for a king.
First Part of Henry VI. Act V. Sc. 5.

All tongues speak of him, and the bleared sights are spectacled to see him.
Coriolanus, Act II. Sc. 1.

December 2.

But we all are men
In our own natures frail, and capable
Of our flesh; few are angels.
Henry VIII. Act V. Sc. 3.

I am not of that feather to shake off
My friend when he must need me.
Timon of Athens, Act I. Sc. 1.

December 3.

Speak freely what you think.
Third Part of Henry VI. Act IV. Sc. 1.

Be just, and fear not:
Let all the ends thou aim'st at be thy country's,
Thy God's, and truth's; then if thou fall'st, . . .
Thou fall'st a blessed martyr!
Henry VIII. Act III. Sc. 2.

December 1.

December 2.

December 3.

December 4.

He hath a stern look, but a gentle heart.
King John, Act IV. Sc. 1.

Let's teach ourselves that honourable stop,
Not to outsport discretion.
Othello, Act II. Sc. 3.

December 5.

Silence is the perfectest herald of joy: I were but little happy, if I could say how much.
Much Ado about Nothing, Act II. Sc. 1.

In all external grace you have some part;
But you like none, none you, for constant heart.
Sonnet LIII.

December 6.

He hath never fed on the dainties that are bred in a book. *Love's Labour's Lost*, Act IV. Sc. 2.

You should be ruled and led
By some discretion, that discerns your state
Better than you yourself. . . . To wilful men,
The injuries that they themselves procure
Must be their schoolmasters.
King Lear, Act II. Sc. 4.

December 4.

December 5.

December 6.

December 7.

Ceremony was but devised at first
To set a gloss on faint deeds, hollow welcomes,
Recanting goodness, sorry ere 'tis shown;
But where there is true friendship, there needs none.
Timon of Athens, Act I. Sc. 2.

In winter's tedious nights sit by the fire with good old folks.
Richard II. Act V. Sc. 1.

December 8.

Hearing you praised, I say, ' 'Tis so, 'tis true,'
And to the most of praise add something more.
Sonnet LXXXV.

Me, poor man, my library were dukedom large enough.
Tempest, Act I. Sc. 2.

December 9.

Heat not a furnace for your foe so hot
That it do singe yourself: we may outrun,
By violent swiftness, that which we run at,
And lose by over-running.
Henry VIII. Act I. Sc. 1.

You shall have time to wrangle in when you have nothing else to do.
Antony and Cleopatra, Act II. Sc. 2.

December 7.

December 8.

December 9.

―――― *December 10.* ――――

I hear, yet say not much, but think the more.
Third Part of Henry VI. Act IV. Sc. 1.

Angels are bright still, though the brightest fell.
Macbeth, Act IV. Sc. 3.

―――― *December 11.* ――――

Rather bear those ills we have,
Than fly to others that we know not of.
Hamlet, Act III. Sc. 1.

Our very eyes are sometimes, like our judgments, blind.
Cymbeline, Act IV. Sc. 2.

. . . . I am declined
Into the vale of years.
Othello, Act III. Sc. 3.

―――― *December 12.* ――――

Doubting things go ill often hurts more
Than to be sure they do; for certainties
Either are past remedies, or, timely knowing,
The remedy then born.
Cymbeline, Act I. Sc. 6.

I hourly learn a doctrine of obedience.
Antony and Cleopatra, Act V. Sc. 2.

December 10.

December 11.

December 12.

―― *December 13.* ――

There is some soul of goodness in things evil,
Would men observingly distil it out.
Henry V. Act IV. Sc. I.

Ween you of better luck,
I mean in perjured witness, than your master,
Whose minister you are, whiles here he lived
Upon this naughty earth.
Henry VIII. Act V. Sc. I.

―― *December 14.* ――

Add a royal number to the dead.
King John, Act II. Sc. 2.

He gave his honours to the world again,
His blessed part to Heaven, and slept in peace.
Henry VIII. Act IV. Sc. 2.

Say as you think, and speak it from your souls.
Second Part of Henry VI. Act III. Sc. I.

―― *December 15.* ――

. . . . I might call him
A thing divine, for nothing natural
I ever saw so noble.
Tempest, Act I. Sc. 2.

All may be well; but, if God sort it so,
'Tis more than we deserve, or I expect.
Richard III. Act II. Sc. 3.

Take from my mouth the wish of happy years.
Richard II. Act I. Sc. 3.

December 13.

December 14.

December 15.

December 16.

He's honest, on mine honour.
Henry VIII. Act v. Sc. 1.

Beshrew me but I love her heartily;
For she is wise, if I can judge of her;
And fair she is, if that mine eyes be true;
And true she is, as she hath proved herself;
And therefore, like herself, wise, fair, and true,
Shall she be placed in my constant soul.
Merchant of Venice, Act II. Sc. 6.

December 17.

For mine own part, I could be well content
To entertain the lag-end of my life
With quiet hours.
First Part of Henry IV. Act v. Sc. 1.

Redeeming time when men think least I will.
First Part of Henry IV. Act I. Sc. 2.

December 18.

You shall hear from me still; the time shall not
Out-go my thinking on you.
Antony and Cleopatra, Act III. Sc. 2.

How like a winter hath my absence been
From thee, the pleasure of the fleeting year!
What freezings have I felt, what dark days seen!
What old December's bareness everywhere!
And yet this time removed was summer's time.
Sonnet XCVII.

December 16.

December 17.

December 18.

December 19.

And he is one,
The truest manner'd ; such a holy witch
That he enchants societies into him ;
Half all men's hearts are his. . . .

Cymbeline, Act I. Sc. 6.

Time comes stealing on by night and day.

Comedy of Errors, Act IV. Sc. 2.

December 20.

We must not stint
Our necessary actions, in the fear
To cope malicious censurers.

Henry VIII. Act I. Sc. 2.

A virtuous and a Christian-like conclusion,
To pray for them that have done scathe to us.

Richard III. Act I. Sc. 3.

December 21.

The web of our life is of a mingled yarn, good and ill together.

All's Well that Ends Well, Act IV. Sc. 3.

Jog on, jog on, the foot-path way,
And merrily hent the stile-a :
A merry heart goes all the day,
Your sad tires in a mile-a.

Winter's Tale, Act IV. Sc. 3.

December 19.

December 20.

December 21.

December 22.

Cease to lament for that thou canst not help,
And study help for that which thou lament'st.
Two Gentlemen of Verona, Act III. Sc. 1.

.... For his bounty
There was no winter in't, an autumn 'twas
That grew the more by reaping.
Antony and Cleopatra, Act V. Sc. 2.

December 23.

O Lord, that lends me life,
Lend me a heart replete with thankfulness!
Second Part of Henry VI. Act I. Sc. 1.

Cold snow melts with the sun's hot beams.
Second Part of Henry VI. Act III. Sc. 1.

December 24.

Look, what thy soul holds dear, imagine it
To lie that way thou go'st, not whence thou comest.
Richard II. Act I. Sc. 3.

Some say that ever 'gainst that season comes,
Wherein our Saviour's birth is celebrated,
The bird of dawning singeth all night long,
And then they say no spirit stirs abroad.
Hamlet, Act I. Sc. 1.

December 22.

December 23.

December 24.

―――――― *December 25.* ――――――

(Christmas Day.)

Alas, alas!
Why, all the souls that were were forfeit once;
And He that might the vantage best have took,
Found out the remedy.
Measure for Measure, Act II. Sc. 2.

The yearly course that brings this day about
Shall never see it but a holiday.
King John, Act III. Sc. 1.

―――――― *December 26.* ――――――

Therefore my age is as a lusty winter,
Frosty, but kindly.
As You Like It, Act II. Sc. 3.

To Thee I do commend my watchful soul,
Ere I let fall the windows of mine eyes:
Sleeping and waking, O, defend me still!
Richard III. Act V. Sc. 3.

―――――― *December 27.* ――――――

Pray you, bid
These unknown friends to's welcome; for it is
The way to make us better friends, more known.
Winter's Tale, Act IV. Sc. 4.

There's rosemary, that's for remembrance.
Hamlet, Act IV. Sc. 6.

December 25.

December 26.

December 27.

December 28.

. . . . So we'll live
And pray, and sing, and tell old tales.
King Lear, Act V. Sc. 2.

Poor Tom's a-cold!
King Lear, Act III. Sc. 4.

December 29.

We see which way the stream of time doth run,
And are enforced from our most quiet there
By the rough torrent of occasion.
Second Part of Henry IV. Act IV. Sc. 1.

Be thou chaste as ice, as pure as snow,
Thou shalt not escape calumny.
Hamlet, Act III. Sc. 1.

December 30.

He sits high in all the people's hearts.
Julius Cæsar, Act I. Sc. 3.

Our hearts,
Of brothers' temper, do receive you in
With all kind love, good thoughts, and reverence.
. . . Though last, not least in love.
Julius Cæsar, Act III. Sc. 1.

December 28.

December 29.

December 30.

December 31.

But with the word the time will bring on summer,
When briers shall have leaves as well as thorns,
And be as sweet as sharp. We must away;
Our waggon is prepared, and time revives us :
All's well that ends well : still the fine's the crown ;
Whate'er the course, the end is the renown.
All's Well that Ends Well, Act IV. Sc. 4.

And time, that takes survey of all the world, must have a stop.
First Part of Henry IV. Act V. Sc. 4.

Parting is such sweet sorrow
That I shall say good-night till it be morrow.
Romeo and Juliet, Act II. Sc. 3.

Then let us take a ceremonious leave
And loving farewell of our several friends.
Richard II. Act I. Sc. 3.

God be with you all !
Henry V. Act IV. Sc. 3.

December 31.

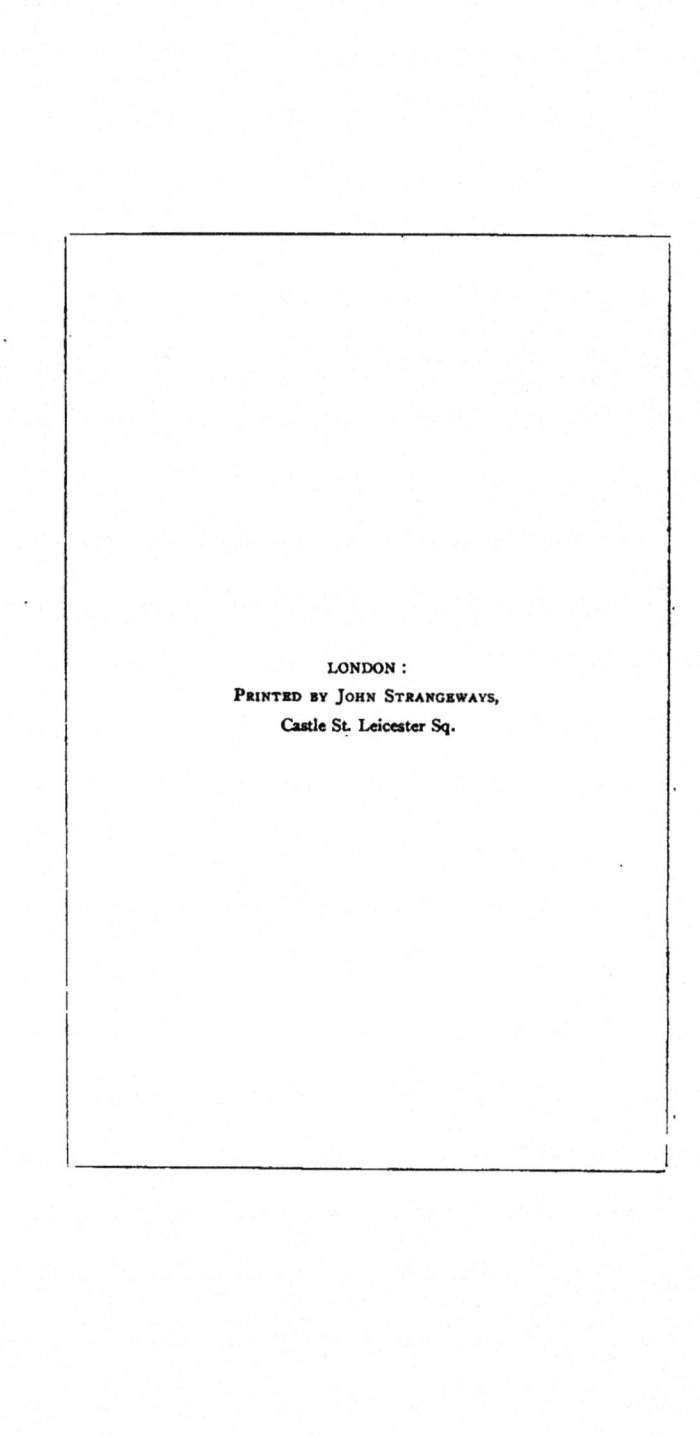

LONDON:
PRINTED BY JOHN STRANGEWAYS,
Castle St. Leicester Sq.